EPIGRAPHICAL NOTES ON GREEK COINAGE

OPERA SELECTA
OF OUR CENTURY'S
CLASSICAL SCHOLARS

I. *MARCVS NIEBVHR TOD:*
THE PROGRESS OF GREEK EPIGRAPHY 1914—1936. (In Preparation).

THE PROGRESS OF GREEK EPIGRAPHY 1937—1953. ISBN 0-89005-292-1. pp. vi + 256 . . . . $30.

ANCIENT GREEK NUMERICAL SYSTEMS. ISBN 0-89005-290-5. pp. vii + 128 . . . . $20.

GREEK INSCRIPTIONS FROM EGYPT 1912—1947. AN ANNOTATED BIBLIOGRAPHY. ISBN 0-89005-293-X . . . . $15.

EPIGRAPHICAL NOTES ON GREEK COINAGE. ISBN 0-89005-319-7. pp. 116 . . . . $15.

II. *THOMAS ALLAN BRADY* (1902—1964):
SARAPIS AND ISIS. Collected Essays. ISBN 0-89005-253-0. pp. xii + 129 . . . . $25.

III. *CARL A. ROEBUCK:*
ECONOMY AND SOCIETY IN THE EARLY GREEK WORLD. Collected Essays.
ISBN 0-89005-261-1. pp. xvi + 162 . . . . $25.

Ares Publishers has produced a new series, the *OPERA SELECTA* of this century's classical scholars, i.e., collections of important articles by leading classical scholars. Additional volumes are already in preparation.

ARES PUBLISHERS INC.
612 N. Michigan Ave., S., 216
Chicago, Illinois 60611

EPIGRAPHICAL NOTES ON GREEK COINAGE

By

M.N. TOD

WITH A PREFATORY NOTE
By
JOSEPH BRESLIN

ARES PUBLISHERS INC.
CHICAGO   MCMLXXIX

© 1979 New Material
A volume formed from uniting
a pamphlet and off-prints
of the original articles
published between the years:
1940-1960
ARES PUBLISHERS INC.
612 N. Michigan Ave., S., 216
Chicago, Illinois 60611
Printed in the United States of America
International Standard Book Number
0-89005-319-7

PREFATORY NOTE

Marcus Tod in a series of articles entitled, "Epigraphical Notes On Greek Coinage," which appeared in *Numismatic Chronicle* between 1945-1960 assembled and evaluated the evidence provided by Greek inscriptions for the study of Greek coins. Tod, the noted epigraphist, found that numismatists passed over epigraphical evidence when studying a particular coin. In *N.C.* ser.6 (1947) 47 Tod wrote: "My impression that students of antiquity are tempted in this age of specialization to work too much in watertight compartments is confirmed by the discovery that of the articles in *RE* on *Chalkus* (Kubitschek), *Dichalkon* (Hultsch), *Trichalkon* (Schwabacher), and *Tetrachalkon* (Regling) three make no reference at all to inscriptions.... Nor do I find a single allusion to any inscription in the articles on these same four words contributed by that distinguished numismatist K. Regling to F. von Schrotter's *Wörterbuch der Munzkunde.*" Tod began with a study of the epigraphical evidence for the κόλλυβος (*N.C.* ser.6, vol.5, 1945, 108-116) and continued his work on three other coins, the Χαλκοῦς (*N.C.* vol.6, 1946, 47-62), the ὀβολὸς (*N.C.* vol.7, 1947, 1-27; *N.C.* vol.15, 1955, 125-130), and finally the δραχμὴ (*N.C.* vol. 20, 1960, 1-24). While these are studies of particular coins, they are also an outgrowth of Tod's work on Greek numerical systems[1].

The Editors at Ares have decided to bring together these important articles[2] between two covers and also to reproduce the pamphlet issued by Tod's friends and colleagues on his seventieth birthday. This pamphlet included Tod's bibliography up to the year 1948 which we have augmented with *addenda* up to the year 1960 from *L'Année Philologique.*

August 1979

Joseph Breslin

---

[1] Cf. *Ancient Greek Numerical Systems, Six Studies by Marcus Niebuhr Tod.* Ares Publishers, Spring 1979

[2] Cf. J. and L. Robert's comments in *Révue des Études Grecques.*, 1949, p. 98.

AN ADDRESS PRESENTED TO

MARCUS NIEBUHR TOD

ON HIS

SEVENTIETH BIRTHDAY

with a Bibliography of
his Writings

Ἀγαθῆι τύχηι

Ἔτους χιλιοστοῦ ἐνακοσιοστοῦ τεσσαρακοστοῦ ὀγδόου, βασιλεύοντος Γεωργίου τοῦ Γεωργίου, ἔδοξε τοῖς συνεργοῖς καὶ φίλοις τοῖς ὑπογεγραμμένοις. ἐπειδὴ Μᾶρκος Ἰωάννου, ὁ ἐπιφανέστατος προστάτης αὐτῶν, ἀνὴρ ἀγαθὸς ὢν καὶ εὔνους καὶ ἐπιεικὴς διατελεῖ περὶ τὸ κοινὸν τῶν τὴν ἐπιγραφικὴν σπουδαζόντων, καὶ φιλανθρώπως διακείμενος τοῖς ἐντυγχάνουσιν εὐεργέτης γίγνεται ἐν πάσαις ταῖς χρείαις εἰς ἃς ἄν τις αὐτὸν παρακαλῇ· δεδόχθαι τοῖς φίλοις ἐπαινέσαι Μᾶρκον ἀρετῆς ἕνεκα καὶ προθυμίας καὶ τιμῆσαι αὐτὸν τὰ γενέθλια ἑστιῶσι τῇ ἀναθέσει τοῦδε τοῦ βιβλίου, καὶ κελεύειν αὐτὸν ὑγιαίνειν καὶ πάντα εὐτυχεῖν, ἵνα εἰδῇ ὅσην ἔχουσι πρὸς αὐτὸν εὔνοιαν καὶ φιλοστοργίαν.

F. E. ADCOCK
A. ANDREWES
FRANCES M. AUSTIN
E. A. BARBER
J. D. BEAZLEY
H. I. BELL
C. M. BOWRA
P. A. BRUNT
W. H. BUCKLER
ARCHIBALD CAMERON
M. CARY
M. P. CHARLESWORTH
G. N. CLARK
J. M. R. CORMACK
A. D. CROW
CHRISTO M. DANOV
GEORGES DAUX

3

STERLING DOW
GLANVILLE DOWNEY
T. J. DUNBABIN
R. H. DUNDAS
C. F. EDSON
VICTOR EHRENBERG
EDWARD S. FORSTER
PETER FRASER
P. FRIEDLAENDER
A. W. GOMME
JOHN G. GRIFFITH
MARGHERITA GUARDUCCI
B. L. HALLWARD
MILDRED HARTLEY
F. M. HEICHELHEIM
C. HIGNETT
J. J. E. HONDIUS
R. J. HOPPER
LILIAN H. JEFFERY
A. H. M. JONES
V. G. KALLIPOLITIS
JOHN H. KENT
GUENTHER KLAFFENBACH
J. A. O. LARSEN
HUGH LAST
H. L. LORIMER
G. P. S. MACPHERSON
C. I. MAKARONAS
H. M. MARGOLIOUTH
RUSSELL MEIGGS
BENJAMIN D. MERITT
T. B. MITFORD
A. MOMIGLIANO
R. MOUTERDE
JOHN L. MYRES
ARTHUR DARBY NOCK

JAMES H. OLIVER
H. W. PARKE
S. P. PELEKIDES
J. M. PETERSON
AUSTIN LANE POOLE
W. KENDRICK PRITCHETT
A. E. RAUBITSCHEK
V. G. RICH
GISELA M. A. RICHTER
LOUIS ROBERT
D. S. ROBERTSON
DAVID M. ROBINSON
RICHARD ROBINSON
H. J. ROSE
M. ROSTOVTZEFF
H. H. SCULLARD
PERCY SIMPSON
G. H. STEVENSON
C. H. V. SUTHERLAND
RONALD SYME
E. G. TURNER
F. J. VARLEY
F. W. WALBANK
RICHARD WALZER
CHARLES BRADFORD WELLES
ADOLF WILHELM
ARTHUR M. WOODWARD

MARCUS NIEBUHR TOD was born in Highgate, north London, on 24 November 1878, the second son of John Tod and his wife Gertrude (*née* von Niebuhr). He received his early education at Merchant Taylors' School, from which he entered St. John's College, Oxford, as a Scholar in October 1897. He obtained a First Class in Classical Honour Moderations in 1899 and a First Class in the Final Honour School of Literae Humaniores in 1901, and was appointed a Senior Student of the British School at Athens in the same year. In the following year he was made Assistant Director and Librarian of the School, a post which he held for three years, and in the same year was elected a Senior Scholar of St. John's and a Craven Travelling Fellow of Oxford University.

In 1903 Oriel College appointed him to a Fellowship, a position which he held till 1947; he was an Assistant Tutor in Oriel from 1905 to 1914 and a Tutor from 1914 to 1940, being Senior Tutor from 1929 to 1938. He was also Librarian of Oriel from 1923 to 1929 and Vice-Provost from 1934 to 1945. Recently his two colleges have honoured him by election to an Honorary Fellowship, St. John's in 1946 and Oriel in 1947.

He was elected a Corresponding Member of the Imperial German Archaeological Institute in 1906, the year in which he published the *Catalogue of the Sparta Museum* in collaboration with Professor A. J. B. Wace, and in the following year he was appointed University Lecturer in Greek Epigraphy and University Reader in 1927. In 1912 he was awarded the Conington Prize for his work, which was published in the following year under the title *International Arbitration amongst the Greeks*. From 1913 to 1929 he was Secretary of the Oxford University Committee for Classical Archaeology, and from 1919 to 1921 Secretary of the Oxford Committee of the Royal Commission on Oxford and Cambridge Universities.

In the First World War, after part-time service in the Ministry of Labour, followed by duty in the Y.M.C.A. at Dieppe, he served with the Allied Force in Macedonia from 1915 to 1919, first as Officer Interpreter and afterwards in the Intelligence Corps, with the rank of Captain. For his meritorious service he was awarded the O.B.E. and the Croix de Guerre avec palmes, and was thrice mentioned in dispatches. Even the stress of war could not quench his zeal for his favourite study, to which his publications on Macedonian epigraphy in the *Annual of the British School*, vol. xxiii, 1918–19, bear witness.

His *Sidelights on Greek History* appeared in 1932, and in the following year his *Greek Historical Inscriptions*, I, a second edition of which was called for in 1946. His undoubted eminence in his chosen field of study was acknowledged by his election in 1929 as a Fellow of the British Academy, by the Honorary Degree of Litt.D. from Dublin University in 1938, and by the Honorary LL.D. from Edinburgh University in 1948, the year which saw the long-awaited second volume of his *Greek Historical Inscriptions*.

For many years his position as doyen of British epigraphists has been unchallenged, and this is proved not only by the wealth of his original contributions to his subject in British and foreign journals, but also by the fact that he has been chosen to review almost every important work on Greek epigraphy that has appeared in the last four decades. He has also done valuable work in excerpting new books, dissertations, and periodicals relating to Greek epigraphy for the ninth edition of Liddell and Scott, and further fruits of his labours will appear in the projected *Supplement*. Not the least important of his services to learning has been his continuous collaboration as assistant-editor of the *Supplementum Epigraphicum Graecum* since its foundation in 1923.

For more than forty years his periodical surveys of the progress of Greek Epigraphy have been eagerly awaited by his fellow workers in the field of ancient history, and this work has not only won him the respect but affection of scholars all over the world. For not only is Tod a consummate scholar himself, but he has been the cause that good scholarship is in others, as many colleagues can testify, who for many years have gratefully leaned on his wise advice, sought his counsel, and reaped the benefit of his unstinted and generous help and encouragement. There are others, also, whose interests are not specifically epigraphic, the hundreds of Oxford undergraduates of the past forty years, who remember Tod as a teacher, and who recall with gratitude the inspiration they received from his lectures on Greek history. The fervent wish of colleagues and former pupils alike on his seventieth birthday is

χρόνια πολλά!

ABBREVIATIONS

A.M.	*Athenische Mitteilungen*
B.S.A.	*Annual of the British School at Athens*
C.Q.	*Classical Quarterly*
C.R.	*Classical Review*
G.R.	*Greece and Rome*
J.E.A.	*Journal of Egyptian Archaeology*
J.H.S.	*Journal of Hellenic Studies*
J.R.S.	*Journal of Roman Studies*
O.M.	*The Oxford Magazine*
Y.W.	*The Year's Work in Classical Studies*

1902

(With R. C. Bosanquet) Archaeology in Greece. *J.H.S.* xxii. 378–94.

1903

Some Unpublished 'Catalogi Paterarum Argentearum'. *B.S.A.* viii. 197–230.

First Impressions of Athens. *The Anchor Watch*, Jan. 1903, 23–8.

1904

A new Fragment of the '*Edictum Diocletiani*'. *J.H.S.* xxiv. 195–202.

An Unpublished Attic Decree. *B.S.A.* ix. 154–75.

Excavations at Palaikastro, § 10. Hagios Nikolaos, *B.S.A.* ix. 336–43.

(With R. M. Dawkins) Excavations at Palaikastro, § 9. Kouraménos. *B.S.A.* ix. 329–35.

The ΠΑΙΔΙΚΟΣ ΑΓΩΝ at the Festival of Artemis Orthia at Sparta. *A.M.* xxix. 50–6.

1905

Notes and Inscriptions from South-western Messenia. *J.H.S.* xxv. 32–55.

Teams of Ball-players at Sparta. *B.S.A.* x. 63–77.

A New Fragment of the Attic Tribute Lists. *B.S.A.* x. 78–82.

Παρατηρήσεις ἐπί τινων ἐπιγραφῶν ἐκ τοῦ ἱεροῦ τοῦ Ὑπερτελεάτου Ἀπόλλωνος. Ἐφημερὶς Ἀρχαιολογική, 1904, 55–60.

1906

(With A. J. B. Wace) A CATALOGUE OF THE SPARTA MUSEUM. (Clarendon Press.)

Inscriptions from Eumeneia. *B.S.A.* xi. 27–31.

Greek Inscriptions. *Y.W.* 1906, 69–74.

Review of E. S. Roberts and E. A. Gardner, *An Introduction to Greek Epigraphy*, Part II. *The Inscriptions of Attica.* *O.M.* Feb. 14, 1906.

1907

Greek Inscriptions. *Y.W.* 1907, 70–7.

Review of J. Sundwall, *Epigraphische Beiträge zur Sozialpolitischen Geschichte Athens im Zeitalter des Demosthenes.* *C.R.* xxi. 214.

Review of J. Sundwall, *De institutis reipublicae Atheniensium post Aristotelis aetatem commutatis*, I. *C.R.* xxi. 213–14.

Review of A. Wilhelm, *Urkunden dramatischer Aufführungen in Athen.* *C.R.* xxi. 182–3.

Review of *The Annual of the British School at Athens*, xi. *O.M.* Feb. 13, 1907.

1908

Three new ΣΦΑΙΡΕΙΣ-Inscriptions. *B.S.A.* xiii. 212–18.

A Statute of an Attic Thiasos. *B.S.A.* xiii. 329–38.

Greek Inscriptions. *Y.W.* 1908, 81–9.

Review of A. Calderini, *La Manomissione e la condizione dei liberti in Grecia.* *J.H.S.* xxviii. 343–4.

1909

(With J. ff. Baker-Penoyre) Thasos: Inscriptions. *J.H.S.* xxix. 91–102, 250.

Review of W. H. S. Jones, *Malaria and Greek History.* *J.H.S.* xxix. 378.

Review of J. Partsch, *Griechische Bürgschaftsrecht*, I. *J.H.S.* xxix. 378–9.

Review of E. Ziebarth, *Aus dem griechischen Schulwesen.* *J.H.S.* xxix. 381–2.

Articles in *Encyclopaedia Britannica*, 11th edition, on: Agesilaus; Agis I, II, III, IV; Antalcidas; Apella; Archidamus I, II, III, IV, V; Aristodemus; Aristomenes; Brasidas; Clearchus; Cleomenes I, II, III; Demaratus; Ephors; Gerousia; Gylippus; Gythium; Helots; Lacedaemon; Laconia; Leonidas; Leotychides; Lycurgus; Lysander; Messene; Messenia; Nauarchia; Pausanias; Perioeci; Pylos; Sparta; Vaphio.

Greek Inscriptions. *Y.W.* 1909, 71–81.

First Impressions of Athens. *Madras Christian College Magazine*, New series, x. 192–200.

Articles in *The Temple Dictionary of the Bible*, by W. Ewing and J. E. H. Thomson, on: Roman Empire; Rome.

Review of W. Ashburner, Νόμος 'Ροδίων Ναυτικός—*The Rhodian Sea Law*. *O.M.* Jan. 27, 1910.

Review of A. Wilhelm, *Beiträge zur griechischen Inschriftenkunde*. *J.H.S.* xxx. 176–7.

Review of *Mélanges d'histoire ancienne*. *J.H.S.* xxx. 177–8.

Review of M. Croiset, *Aristophanes and the Political Parties at Athens*. *J.H.S.* xxx. 178.

Review of H. Francotte, *Les Finances des cités grecques*. *J.H.S.* xxx. 369–70.

Review of F. Poland, *Geschichte des griechischen Vereinswesens*. *J.H.S.* xxx. 179–80.

Review of H. J. W. Tillyard, *Agathocles*. *J.H.S.* xxx. 179.

Greek Inscriptions. *Y.W.* 1910, 65–76.

Review of C. Phillipson, *The International Law and Custom of Ancient Greece and Rome*. *J.H.S.* xxxi. 128–9.

Review of A. E. Zimmern, *The Greek Commonwealth*. *J.H.S.* xxxi. 317–18.

Review of M. Brillant, *Les Secrétaires athéniens*. *J.H.S.* xxxi. 323.

1912

Thoinarmostria. *J.H.S.* xxxii. 100–4.

Greek Inscriptions. *Y.W.* 1911, 79–89.

(With M. L. Smith) Greek Inscriptions from Asia Minor. *Liverpool Annals*, iv. 35–44.

International Arbitration in the Greek World. *Journal of the Transactions of the Victoria Institute*, xliv. 275–96.

Review of A. Wilhelm, *Beiträge zur griechischen Inschriftenkunde*. *C.R.* xxvi. 13–15.

Review of A. Thumb, *Handbook of the Modern Greek Vernacular*. *O.M.* Oct. 31, 1912.

Review of M. Brillant, *Les Secrétaires athéniens*. *C.R.* xxvi. 233–4.

Review of E. Breccia, *Catalogue Général des Antiquités Égyptiennes du Musée d'Alexandrie: Iscrizioni Greche e Latine*. *J.H.S.* xxxii. 406–7.

1913

INTERNATIONAL ARBITRATION AMONGST THE GREEKS. (Clarendon Press.)

Three Greek Numeral Systems. *J.H.S.* xxxiii. 27–34.

The Greek Numeral Notation. *B.S.A.* xviii. 98–132.

Greek Inscriptions. *Y.W.* 1912, 77–89.

Review of C. D. Buck, *Introduction to the Study of the Greek Dialects*. *J.H.S.* xxxiii. 140–1.

Review of E. Hermann, *Griechische Forschungen*, I. *Die Nebensätze in den griechischen Dialektinschriften*. *J.H.S.* xxxiii. 371.

1914

Notes on *Inscriptiones Graecae*, V. 1. *J.H.S.* xxxiv. 60–3.

The Progress of Greek Epigraphy, 1913–14. *J.H.S.* xxxiv. 321–31.

Bibliography of 1912–13: Greek Inscriptions from Egypt. *J.E.A.* i. 140–3.

Greek Inscriptions. *Y.W.* 1913, 59–67.
Review of S. C. Kaines Smith, *Greek Art and National Life.*
O.M. Feb. 5, 1914.
Review of J. I. Manatt, *Aegean Days. O.M.* May 7, 1914.
Review of O. Kern, *Inscriptiones Graecae. J.H.S.* xxxiv. 342.

1915

The Progress of Greek Epigraphy, 1914–15. *J.H.S.* xxxv.
260–70.
Bibliography: Graeco-Roman Egypt, B. Inscriptions (1914).
J.E.A. ii. 108–12.
Notes on some Inscriptions from Asia Minor. *C.R.* xxix. 1–4.
On an Archaic Thessalian Epigram. *C.R.* xxix. 196–7.
Greek History with Greek Inscriptions. *Y.W.* 1914, 79–93.
Articles in the *International Standard Bible Encyclopaedia* on:
Amphipolis; Apollonia; Beroea; Cyprus; Dalmatia; Illyricum; Macedonia; Neapolis; Paphos; Philippi; Salamis;
Tarsus; Thessalonica.
Chapter on Greek Inscriptions in C. L. Woolley and T. E.
Lawrence, *The Wilderness of Zin. Palestine Exploration
Fund Annual,* iii. 133–45.
Review of A. Elter, *Ein athenisches Gesetz über die eleusinische
Aparche. J.H.S.* xxxv. 154–5.
Review of W. Larfeld, *Griechische Epigraphik,* 3rd edition,
C.R. xxix. 87–9.

1916

Greek History and Inscriptions. *Y.W.* 1915, 49–61.
A Model Army-Contractor. *Balkan News,* April 10, 1916.
Ἡ ἀρχαία πλὰξ τῶν Καπουτζήδων. Νέα Ἀλήθεια, Feb. 3, 1916.
Αἱ ἀρχαιότητες τῆς Θεσσαλονίκης. Μακεδονία, Feb. 24, 1916.

1919

The Progress of Greek Epigraphy, 1915–18. *J.H.S.* xxxix.
209–31.

1920

Bibliography: Graeco-Roman Egypt, B. Greek Inscriptions
(1915–19). *J.E.A.* vi. 214–18.

1921

The Progress of Greek Epigraphy, 1919–20. *J.H.S.* xli. 50–
69.

Bibliography: Graeco-Roman Egypt, B. Greek Inscriptions
(1920). *J.E.A.* vii. 105–6.

Review of P. Foucart, *Un décret athénien relatif aux com-
battants de Phylé*. *C.R.* xxxv. 36–7.

1922

Greek Inscriptions from Macedonia. *J.H.S.* xlii. 167–83.

Recently Discovered Records of Ancient Cures. *Proceedings
of the Royal Society of Medicine*, 1922, vol. xv (*Section of
the History of Medicine*), 24–6.

1923

The Progress of Greek Epigraphy, 1921–22. *J.H.S.* xliii.
11–39.

Macedonia, VI. Inscriptions. *B.S.A.* xxiii. 67–97, 110–11.

The Macedonian Era, I. *B.S.A.* xxiii. 206–17.

Bibliography (1921–1922): Graeco-Roman Egypt, Greek Inscriptions. *J.E.A.* ix. 235–8.

1924

The Macedonian Era, II. *B.S.A.* xxiv. 54–67.

Three Notes on Appian. *C.Q.* xviii. 99–104.

Review of *Anatolian Studies presented to Sir William Mitchell
Ramsay*, edited by W. H. Buckler and W. M. Calder.
J.R.S. xii. 291–3.

Review of H. Swoboda, *Zwei Kapitel aus dem griechischen
Bundesrecht*. *C.R.* xxxviii. 211.

Review of *Anatolian Studies presented to Sir William Mitchell Ramsay*, edited by W. H. Buckler and W. M. Calder. *O.M.* May 15, 1924.

1925

The Progress of Greek Epigraphy, 1923–24. *J.H.S.* xlv. 102–19, 183–200.

Bibliography (1923–1924): Greek Inscriptions. *J.E.A.* xi. 327–30.

Notes on some Greek Graffiti. *J.E.A.* xi. 256–8.

'The Frogs' of Aristophanes. *Oxford High School Magazine*, July 1925.

Review of Rein van der Velde, *Thessalische Dialektgeographie*. *J.H.S.* xlv. 150.

Review of J. J. E. Hondius, *Novae Inscriptiones Atticae*. *J.H.S.* xlv. 289–90.

Review of *The Annual of the British School at Athens*, xxv. *O.M.* June 4, 1925.

1926

Is it the Lex Gabinia? *Proceedings of the Classical Association*, xxiii. 13–14.

1927

The Progress of Greek Epigraphy, 1925–26. *J.H.S.* xlvii. 182–217.

Bibliography (1925–1926): Greek Inscriptions. *J.E.A.* xiii. 247–50.

The Economic Background of the Fifth Century. *Cambridge Ancient History*, v. 1–32, 491–7.

Review of F. Durrbach, *Inscriptions de Délos: Comptes des Hiéropes* (Nos. 290–371). *J.H.S.* xlvii. 160.

Review of R. G. Kent, *The Textual Criticism of Inscriptions*. *J.H.S.* xlvii. 265–6.

Review of D. M. Robinson, *Greek and Latin Inscriptions from Asia Minor*. *J.H.S.* xlvii. 266.

1928

A Forgotten Epigraphist. *J.H.S.* xlviii. 1–6.

A Survey of Laconian Epigraphy, 1913–1925. *B.S.A.* xxvi. 106–15.

Review of R. Laqueur, *Epigraphische Untersuchungen zu den griechischen Volksbeschlüssen.* *J.H.S.* xlviii. 262.

Review of G. M. Calhoun and C. Delamere, *A Working Bibliography of Greek Law.* *C.R.* xlii. 191.

Review of R. Laqueur, *Epigraphische Untersuchungen zu den griechischen Volksbeschlüssen.* *C.R.* xlii. 204–5.

1929

The Progress of Greek Epigraphy, 1927–28. *J.H.S.* xlix. 172–216.

Bibliography: Greek Inscriptions (1927–1928). *J.E.A.* xv. 259–61.

Further Notes on the Greek Acrophonic Numerals. *B.S.A.* xxviii. 141–57.

Nugae Epigraphicae. *C.Q.* xxiii. 1–6.

Review of A. Zimmern, *Solon and Croesus and other Greek Essays.* *C.R.* xliii. 128–30.

Review of J. Toutain, *L'Économie antique*, and J. Toutain, *The Economic Life of the Ancient World.* *J.R.S.* xix. 250–1.

1930

A Bronze Mirror in the Ashmolean Museum. *J.H.S.* l. 32–6.

Review of A. M. Andreades, Ἱστορία τῆς Ἑλληνικῆς Δημοσίας Οἰκονομίας, I, II (1). *The Economic Journal*, xl. 686–8.

Review of L. Jalabert and R. Mouterde, *Inscriptions grecques et latines de la Syrie*, I. *J.H.S.* l. 152–3.

Review of F. Solmsen–E. Fraenkel, *Inscriptiones Graecae ad inlustrandas dialectos selectae.* *J.H.S.* l. 351.

Review of F. Durrbach, *Inscriptions de Délos: Comptes des*

Hiéropes (Nos. 372–498), *Lois ou Règlements, Contrats d'Entreprises et Devis* (Nos. 499–509). *J.H.S.* l. 351–2.

Review of A. Ferrabino, *La dissoluzione della libertà nella Grecia Antica.* *C.R.* xliv. 41–2.

Review of N. S. Valmin, *Inscriptions de la Messénie.* *C.R.* xliv. 89.

1931

The Progress of Greek Epigraphy, 1929–30. *J.H.S.* li. 211–55.

1932

SIDELIGHTS ON GREEK HISTORY. (Oxford.)

Bibliography: Greek Inscriptions (1929–1930). *J.E.A.* xviii. 105–7.

Greek Inscriptions, I. A New Record of the Attic Drama. *G.R.* i. 114–16.

Greek Inscriptions, II. An Unrecorded Visit of the Scipios to Crete. *G.R.* i. 163–5.

Greek Inscriptions, III. The Bequest of Cyrene to Rome. *G.R.* ii. 47–51.

Review of B. D. Meritt, *Corinth,* VIII (1), *Greek Inscriptions, 1896–1927.* *C.R.* xlvi. 63–4.

1933

A SELECTION OF GREEK HISTORICAL INSCRIPTIONS TO THE END OF THE FIFTH CENTURY B.C. (Clarendon Press.)

An Unpublished Epigram in Oxford. *J.H.S.* liii. 54–6.

The Progress of Greek Epigraphy, 1931–32. *J.H.S.* liii. 214–65.

Bibliography: Greek Inscriptions (1931–1932). *J.E.A.* xix. 185–8.

Greek Inscriptions, IV. A Spartan Grave on Attic Soil. *G.R.* ii. 108–11.

Greek Inscriptions, V. A Recently Discovered Attic Sanctuary. *G.R.* ii. 175–7.

Greek Inscriptions, VI. A Hymn to Pan. *G.R.* iii. 49–52.

A Greek Epigram from Gaza. *Aegyptus*, xiii. 152–8.

Review of W. A. Laidlaw, A History of Delos. *O.M.* Oct. 12, 1933.

1934

Greek Inscriptions at Cairness House. *J.H.S.* liv. 140–62.

Review of M. Hartge, *Griechische Steinschriften als Ausdruck lebendigen Geistes. J.H.S.* liv. 93.

Review of G. Daux and A. Salač, *Fouilles de Delphes.* Tome III. *Épigraphie*, Fasc. iii. *J.H.S.* liv. 94.

Review of A. Dain, *Inscriptions grecques du Musée du Louvre: les textes inédits. J.H.S.* liv. 217–18.

Review of W. H. Buckler and D. M. Robinson, *Sardis*, VII. *Greek and Latin Inscriptions. C.R.* xlviii. 68–9.

1935

The Progress of Greek Epigraphy, 1933–34. *J.H.S.* lv. 172–223.

Bibliography, Part II, Greek Inscriptions (1933–1934). *J.E.A.* xxi. 104–7.

A Greek Epitaph from Jaffa. *Palestine Exploration Fund: Quarterly Statement*, lxvii (1935), 85–6.

Review of É. Bourguet, *Fouilles de Delphes.* Tome III, *Épigraphie*, Fasc. v. *J.H.S.* lv. 92–3.

Review of F. Durrbach and P. Roussel, *Inscriptions de Délos: Actes des fonctionnaires athéniens préposés à l'administration des sanctuaires après 166 av. J.-C.* (Nos. 1400–1479); *Fragments d'actes divers* (Nos. 1480–1496). *J.H.S.* lv. 250–1.

Review of K. Hanell, *Megarische Studien. C.R.* xlix. 76–7.

Review of J. Kirchner, *Imagines Inscriptionum Atticarum. C.R.* xlix. 227–8.

Review of P. Graindor, *Athènes sous Hadrien. J.R.S.* xxv. 250–1.

1936

Chapter on Greek Inscriptions in C. L. Woolley and T. E. Lawrence, *The Wilderness of Zin*, 2nd edition.

Review of *Inscriptiones Graecae*: Vol. II et III *editio minor*, Pars iii, fasc. prior, edited by J. Kirchner. *J.H.S.* lvi. 256.

Review of K. Hanell, *Die Inschriftensammlung des Konstantinos Laskaris*. *C.R.* l. 39.

Review of M. Dunand, *Le Musée de Soueïda*. *Journal of the Royal Asiatic Society*, 1936, 357–9.

1937

The Progress of Greek Epigraphy, 1935–36. *J.H.S.* lvii. 160–218.

Bibliography: Graeco-Roman Egypt, Part II. Greek Inscriptions (1935–1936). *J.E.A.* xxiii. 106–9.

1938

Notes on Attic Inventories. *J.H.S.* lviii. 97–8.

Review of P. Roussel and M. Launey, *Inscriptions de Délos: Décrets postérieurs à 166 av. J.-C.* (Nos. 1497–1524); *Dédicaces postérieures à 166 av. J.-C.* (Nos. 1525–2219), and *Inscriptions de Délos: Dédicaces postérieures à 166 av. J.-C.* (Nos. 2220–2528); *Textes divers, listes et catalogues, fragments divers postérieurs à 166 av. J.-C.* (Nos. 2529–2879). *J.H.S.* lviii. 281.

Review of C. J. Cadoux, *Ancient Smyrna*. *O.M.* October 20, 1938.

Review of B. D. Meritt, *Documents on Athenian Tribute*. *C.R.* lii. 138–9.

Review of S. Dow, *Prytaneis*. *C.R.* lii. 204.

1939

The Progress of Greek Epigraphy, 1937–38. *J.H.S.* lix. 241–81.

Bibliography: Graeco-Roman Egypt, Part II. Greek Inscriptions (1937–1938). *J.E.A.* xxv. 89–93.

The Scorpion in Graeco-Roman Egypt. *J.E.A.* xxv. 55–61.

The *Corrector* Maximus. *Anatolian Studies presented to William Hepburn Buckler*, 333–44.

Review of B. D. Meritt, H. T. Wade-Gery, and M. F. McGregor, *The Athenian Tribute Lists*, I. *J.H.S.* lix. 300–1.

Review of L. Robert, *Collection Froehner*, I. *Inscriptions grecques*. *J.H.S.* lix. 301–2.

Review of B. Bagatti, *Il cimitero di Commodilla o dei Martiri Felice e Adautto presso la Via Ostiense*, and of A. Prandi, *La Memoria Apostolorum in Catacumbas*, I. *Illustrazione del rilievo e studio architettonico del complesso monumentale*. *Journal of Theological Studies*, xl. 436–7.

1940

The Greek Acrophonic Numerals. *B.S.A.* xxxvii. 236–58.

Review of L. Jalabert and R. Mouterde, *Inscriptions grecques et latines de la Syrie*, II. *J.H.S.* lx. 113–14.

Review of H. Michell, *The Economics of Ancient Greece*. *History*, xxv. 252–3.

1941

A Greek Epigram from Egypt. *J.E.A.* xxvii. 99–105.

Bibliography: Graeco-Roman Egypt; Greek Inscriptions (1939–1940). *J.E.A.* xxvii. 153–6.

Big Game Hunters in Ptolemaic and Roman Libya. *J.E.A.* xxvii. 159–60.

Bithynica. *American Journal of Philology*, lxii. 191–8.

History in Stone. *The Guardian*, Feb. 21, 1941.

Review of E. Groag, *Die römischen Reichsbeamten von Achaia bis auf Diokletian*. *J.R.S.* xxxi. 178–9.

1942

An Epigraphical Note-book of Sir Arthur Evans. *J.H.S.* lxi. 39.

Lexicographical Notes. *Hermathena*, lix. 67–93, lx. 16–37.

A Bilingual Dedication from Alexandria. *J.E.A.* xxviii. 53–6.

Review of J. H. Oliver, *The Sacred Gerusia.* *C.R.* lvi. 85–6.

1943

The Progress of Greek Epigraphy, 1939–40. *J.H.S.* lxii. 51–83.

Review of M. Avi-Yonah, *Abbreviations in Greek Inscriptions: The Near East, 200 B.C.–A.D. 1100. J.H.S.* lxii. 89.

Review of G. Tsereteli, *A Bilingual Inscription from Armazi near Mcheta in Georgia. J.R.S.* xxxiii. 82–6.

Review of J. Day, *An Economic History of Athens under Roman Domination. J.R.S.* xxxiii. 105–7.

Review of B. D. Meritt, *Epigraphica Attica. J.R.S.* xxxiii. 119–20.

1945

A Greek Inscription from the Persian Gulf. *J.H.S.* lxiii. 112–13.

Retrospect. *The Glory that is Greece*, edited by H. Hughes, 146–50.

1946

A SELECTION OF GREEK HISTORICAL INSCRIPTIONS TO THE END OF THE FIFTH CENTURY B.C., 2nd edition. (Clarendon Press.)

A Note on the Spelling ἐξάμου = ἐκ Σάμου. *American Journal of Philology*, lxvii. 329–33.

(With R. P. Austin) Athens and the Satraps' Revolt. *J.H.S.* lxiv. 98–100.

Bibliography: Graeco-Roman Egypt. Greek Inscriptions (1941–1945). *J.E.A.* xxxi. 101–4.

Review of N. Valmin, *Fouilles de Delphes*, III. 6, G. Daux, *Fouilles de Delphes*, III. 3 (2), and G. Daux, *Chronologie delphique. J.H.S.* lxiv. 114–15.

Review of M. Feyel, *Contribution à l'épigraphie béotienne. C.R.* lx. 87–8.

The Progress of Greek Epigraphy, 1941–45. *J.H.S.* lxv. 58–99.

Epigraphical Notes on Greek Coinage, I. ΚΟΛΛΥΒΟΣ. *Numismatic Chronicle*, 1945, 108–16.

Epigraphical Notes on Greek Coinage, II. ΧΑΛΚΟΥΣ. *Numismatic Chronicle*, 1946, 47–62.

Review of W. A. Wigram, *Hellenic Travel: a Guide*. *O.M.* Nov. 6, 1947.

1948

A SELECTION OF GREEK HISTORICAL INSCRIPTIONS FROM 403 TO 323 B.C. (Clarendon Press.)

Epigraphical Notes on Greek Coinage, III. ΟΒΟΛΟΣ. *Numismatic Chronicle*, 1947, 1–27.

In the press

The Progress of Greek Epigraphy, 1945–47. *J.H.S.*

Bibliography: Graeco-Roman Egypt. Greek Inscriptions (1945–1947). *J.E.A.* xxxiv.

Oxford Classical Dictionary, articles on Arbitration; Clubs; Epigraphy; Marmor Parium.

Chambers' Encyclopaedia, article on Epigraphy.

For ADDENDA to the Bibliography
of M.N. Tod. see p. 29-30

COMPARATIO NUMERORUM OF PAGE NUMBERS
BETWEEN THE ORIGINAL ARTICLES AND THIS EDITION:
(*pages of this Edition in italics*)

Numismatic Chronicle
1945, ser.6, vol.5

108 = *32*
109 = *33*
110 = *34*
111 = *35*
112 = *36*
113 = *37*
114 = *38*
115 = *39*
116 = *40*

1946, ser.6, vol.6

47 = *41*
48 = *42*
49 = *43*
50 = *44*
51 = *45*
52 = *46*
53 = *47*
54 = *48*
55 = *49*
56 = *50*
57 = *51*
58 = *52*
59 = *53*
60 = *54*
61 = *55*
62 = *56*

1947, ser.6, vol.7

1 = *57*
2 = *58*
3 = *59*

1947, ser.6, vol. 7

4 = *60*
5 = *61*
6 = *62*
7 = *63*
8 = *64*
9 = *65*
10 = *66*
11 = *67*
12 = *68*
13 = *69*
14 = *70*
15 = *71*
16 = *72*
17 = *73*
18 = *74*
19 = *75*
20 = *76*
21 = *77*
22 = *78*
23 = *79*
24 = *80*
25 = *81*
26 = *82*

Numismatic Chronicle
1955, ser.6, vol.15

125 = *85*
126 = *86*
127 = *87*
128 = *88*
129 = *89*
130 = *90*

1960, ser.6, vol.20

1 = *93*
2 = *94*
3 = *95*
4 = *96*
5 = *97*
6 = *98*
7 = *99*
8 = *100*
9 = *101*
10 = *102*
11 = *103*
12 = *104*
13 = *105*
14 = *106*
15 = *107*
16 = *108*
17 = *109*
18 = *110*
19 = *111*
20 = *112*
21 = *113*
22 = *114*
23 = *115*
24 = *116*

CONTENTS

ADDENDA 1947-1960

1947

The Progress of Greek Epigraphy, 1945-1947. *JHS* 67 (1947) 90-127.

1948

Bibliography: Graeco-Roman Egypt. Greek Inscriptions, 1945-1947. *JEA* 1948, 109-113.

1949

Epigraphical Notes, *AJP* 1949, 113-117.

Greek Record-Keeping and Record Breaking. *CQ* 1949, 106-112.

1950

Bibliography: Graeco-Roman Egypt. Greek Inscriptions, 1948-1949. *JEA* 36 (1950) 106-109.

The Alphabetic Numeral System In Attica. *BSA* 45 (1950) 126-139.

Epigraphical Notes On Freedmen's Professions. *Epigraphica* 12 (1950) 3-26.

1951

A Teetotaller's Epitaph. *Hermathena* 77 (1951) 20-24.

An Ephebic Inscription From Memphis. *JEA* 37 (1951) 86-99.

Epigraphical Notes From The Ashmolean Museum. *JHS* 71 (1951) 172-177.

Laudatory Epithets In Greek Epitaphs. *BSA* 46 (1951) 182-190.

1952

The Progress of Greek Epigraphy, 1948-1949. *JHS* 72 (1952) 20-55.

Notes On Some Inscriptions From Kalyvia Sokhas. *BSA* 47 (1952) 118-122.

1953

M.N. Tod., D.E.L. Haynes, An Inscribed Marble Portrait-Herm In The British Museum. *JHS* 73 (1953) 138-140.

The Macedonian Era Reconsidered: *Studies Presented to D.M. Robinson II*, 382-397, Washington Univ. St. Louis, Mo. 1953.

1954

The Progress of Greek Epigraphy, 1950-1951. *JHS* 74 (1954) 59-84.

Letter-Labels In Greek Inscriptions. *BSA* 49 (1954) 1-8.

1955

The Rhoummas Herm. A Postscript. *JHS* 75 (1955) 155.

The Progress of Greek Epigraphy, 1952-1953. *JHS* 75 (1955) 122-152

Epigraphical Notes On Greek Coinage. *Addenda NC* 15 (1955) 125-130.

1956

A New Eleusinian Title? *AJP* 77 (1956) 52-54.

1957

Sidelights On Greek Philosophers. *JHS* 77 (1957) 132-141.

1960

Epigraphical Notes On Greek Coinage. *NC* 20 (1960) 1-24.

EPIGRAPHICAL NOTES ON GREEK COINAGE

EPIGRAPHICAL NOTES ON GREEK COINAGE

In these days of increasing specialization, when there is some danger that the field of scholarship may be divided into rigidly demarcated zones, separated by impenetrable "iron curtains", it may seem rash for one who can make no pretension to be a numismatist to offer some suggestions in the pages of this *Chronicle*. Nevertheless, I am encouraged to do so by Dr. C. H. V. Sutherland and by Mr. E. S. G. Robinson, to whom I express my warm thanks for their kindness in reading the following note in manuscript and making some valuable suggestions.

I. ΚΟΛΛΥΒΟΣ

The word κόλλυβος (together with its derivates κολλυβιστής, κολλυβιστικός, κολλυβιστήριον) is well attested in literature, inscriptions, and papyri, and examples are cited in Liddell and Scott's *Greek Lexicon* ranging from the fifth century B.C. to the second A.D.

Κολλυβιστής, though used by Lysias and Menander, was censured as non-Attic by Phrynichus (κολλυβιστὴς ἐπὶ τοῦ ἀργυραμοιβοῦ. πάλιν ἡμᾶς μολύνων οὐδέν τι ἀναπαύεται ὁ Μένανδρος. ὁ μὲν γὰρ κόλλυβος δόκιμον, τὸ δὲ κολλυβιστὴς ἀδόκιμον), by Moeris (ἀργυραμοιβοὶ Ἀττικῶς· κολλυβισταὶ Ἑλληνικῶς) and by Thomas Magister (ed. Ritschl, p. 203 κολλυβιστὴς ἐπὶ τοῦ ἀργυραμοιβοῦ φησιν ὁ Μένανδρος ἀδοκίμως· τὸ μὲν γὰρ κόλλυβος [ὅπερ ἐστὶν εἶδος νομίσματος] δόκιμον, τὸ δὲ κολλυβιστὴς παρασεσημασμένον, and p. 16 ἀργυραμοιβός, οὐ κολλυβιστής). It was in common use in Hellenistic and Roman times to denote a banker or money-changer, the best-known instances being those in the New Testament (Matt. xxi. 12, Mark xi. 15, John ii. 15; in this last passage the word is synonymous with κερματιστής, which occurs in the preceding verse). To the examples cited in Liddell and Scott we may add Moeris and Thomas Magister quoted above, Pollux, vii. 170 τραπεζίτης . . . κολλυβιστής, and Hesychius κολλυβιστής· τραπεζίτης.[1]

To the above-mentioned words must be added the verb κολλυβίζω, omitted from Liddell and Scott, meaning "to cut up into small pieces" or "to give small change". This occurs in the

---

[1] For κολλυβιστικὴ τράπεζα see *Pap. Oxy.*, xii. 1411. 4 with comment, F. Preisigke, *Wörterbuch*, i. 819, *Girowesen im griech. Ägypten*, 32.

scholiast on Aristophanes, *Frogs*, 507, and, in almost the same words, in Suidas κολλάβους· τοὺς ἄρτους τοὺς ἐοικότας τὴν πλάσιν τοῖς κολλάβοις τῆς κιθάρας. οἱ δὲ εἶδος πλακοῦντος τετραγώνου, ἢ ἄρτου μικροῦ· παρὰ τὸ ἐκ μεγάλων κολλυβίζεσθαι,[2] and also in Origen, who uses the word both transitively (ἀργύρια κολλυβίζοντες, *Patrol. Graec.* xiii. 1444 C) and intransitively (*ibid.*, 1448 A).

Κόλλυβος appears as an unmistakably masculine noun in Theophrastus, *De lap.*, 46, *OGI* 515. 50, Pollux, iii. 84, vii. 170, Hesychius *s.v.* κολλυβιστής, Phrynichus and Thomas Magister, *locc. cit.*, and as a neuter, κόλλυβον, only in Pollux, ix. 72, where the writer may have been misled by the compounds δικόλλυβον, τρικόλλυβον, or, more probably, by the heteroclite plural found in Origen (διδόντες κόλλυβα τοῖς προσιοῦσιν, iv. 191 B) and in Hesychius, κόλλυβα· τρωγάλια. The word bears three principal meanings:

(1) The plural, κόλλυβοι or κόλλυβα, denotes one kind of τραγήματα, such as were used to welcome a fresh accession to the slave-household. Hesychius, we have seen, defines κόλλυβα as τρωγάλια, small cakes or pastries, and the scholiast on Aristophanes, *Plutus*, 768, says σύγκειται δὲ τὰ καταχύσματα ἀπὸ φοινίκων, κολλύβων, τρωγαλίων, ἰσχάδων καὶ καρύων, and again, κατέχεον κόλλυβα καὶ ἰσχάδας καὶ φοίνικας καὶ τρωγάλια καὶ ἄλλα τραγήματα, while in the foundation-charter of the guild of worshippers of Men Tyrannus, instituted at Sunium in the second or third century of our era, it is provided that παρέξουσιν οἱ ἐρανισταὶ τὰ καθήκοντα τῶι θεῶι . . . καὶ ἐφίερα τρία καὶ κολλύβων χοίνικες (*sic*) δύο (*IG* ii². 1366. 22–4). In a full and valuable paper on the κόλλυβος, read [3] at a meeting of the Académie des Inscriptions et Belles-Lettres on March 30, 1928, and published later in that year in the *Revue Numismatique*, xxxi. 145 ff., Théodore Reinach, apparently on the ground of the distinction drawn by the scholiast between κόλλυβοι and τρωγάλια, dismisses Hesychius' definition κόλλυβα· τρωγάλια as "une glose absurde", and takes the primary meaning of κόλλυβος to be some kind of grain or edible pulse, perhaps a variety of pea, a view already stated by

---

[2] This remains as valid evidence for the existence of a verb κολλυβίζω even if, with Th. Reinach (*Rev. Num.*, xxxi. 146), we reject the connexion between κόλλυβοι and κόλλαβοι. For further examples see the scholiast on Aristophanes, *Peace*, 1196 (κεκολλυβισμένοι), and *Frogs*, 507 (κολλυβίζεσθαι).

[3] See the brief résumé contained in the *Comptes-rendus de l'Académie*, 1928, 110.

K. Regling (Pauly-Wissowa, *R.-E.* xi. 1099). This may be right, though to me it seems strange that no mention should be made of this vegetable in Greek botanical literature, nor does the pea seem quite at home among the succulent dainties—dates, figs, walnuts, and cakes—which compose the Aristophanic καταχύσματα. As regards the derivation of the word, Reinach dismisses the connexion, suggested in Liddell and Scott, with the Hebrew *ḥālap* = "change", "exchange", and denies the possibility of a Greek or Semitic etymology. " Il est probable ", he concludes (p. 160), "que nous avous là, comme pour quantité de noms de plantes, un vocable préhellénique, peut-être asiatique."

(2) More frequent, especially in inscriptions and papyri, is the use of κόλλυβος to denote "agio", "rate of exchange", for which Liddell and Scott cite, in addition to two passages of Cicero and one in a second-century papyrus,[4] two second-century inscriptions, one a decree of Tenos honouring a Syracusan benefactor (*IG* xii (5). 817. 4, [8]), the other a Delphian decree of 162–0 B.C. (*SIG*³ 672) accepting a donation from Attalus II of Pergamum and instituting the festival of the Attalea (cf. G. Daux, *Delphes au IIᵉ et au Iᵉʳ siècle*, 686 ff.), where we read τὰ δὲ ἀναλώμα|τα καὶ ἐφόδια ἐξέστω καταχρεῖσθαι ἐκ τοῦ κολλύβου (l. 31 f.). In the fourth century B.C. we find the term ἐπικαταλλαγά used in Delphian records in this sense (*Fouilles de Delphes*, iii (5). 25 ii A 11 ; 58. 7), reminding us of Pollux, vii. 170 καὶ ὁ νῦν κόλλυβος ἀλλαγή, καὶ τὸ (κολλυβίζειν?) καταλλάττειν τὸ νόμισμα, and iii. 84 ἀργυρίου ἀλλαγὴ ὁ καλούμενος κόλλυβος. Two further inscriptions may here be cited, the rescript addressed to Pergamum by a Roman Emperor, probably Hadrian, which refers to τὴν ἐκ τοῦ κολλύβου πρόσοδον (*OGI* 484. 19),[5] and the famous decree of Mylasa regulating the transactions of bankers (τραπεζῖται) in A.D. 209–11, in which κόλλυβος occurs four times (*OGI* 515. 22, 25, 50, 57).[6] On this sense of κόλλυβος see, further, Reinach, *op. cit.*, 146 ff.

---

[4] The word in this sense is common in papyri ; see F. Preisigke, *Wörterbuch*, iii. 242, *Fachwörter*, 112, and U. Wilcken, *Griech. Ostraka*, i. 381. The adjective [ἀκολ|λ]ύβιστος occurs in *IG* xii (5). 817. 9 f.

[5] Cf. *OGI* ii, p. 552, *IGRom.* iv. 352, F. F. Abbott and A. C. Johnson, *Municipal Administration in the Roman Empire*, 401 ff., no. 81, T. R. S. Broughton in T. Frank, *Economic Survey of Ancient Rome*, iv. 892 ff.

[6] Cf. Abbott and Johnson, *op. cit.*, 461 ff., no. 133, Broughton, *op. cit.*, 895 ff.

(3) We now come to the use of the word to denote a very small coin or weight. This latter meaning is found in Theophrastus, *De lapidibus*, 46, who, speaking of the power of a certain stone to detect even the slightest degree of impurity in gold, says ἐλάχιστον δὲ γίνεται κριθή,[7] εἶτα κόλλυβος, εἶτα τεταρτημόριον (a quarter-obol) ἢ ἡμιώβολος.[8] The former meaning is amply attested. Hesychius (*s.v.* κολλυβιστής) says κόλλυβος γὰρ εἶδος νομίσματος, καὶ ὁ ἐν τῷ χαλκῷ κεχαραγμένος βοῦς,[9] and Pollux, ix. 72, emphasizes its trifling value in his remark εἴη δ' ἂν καὶ κόλλυβον λεπτόν τι νομισμάτιον· Καλλίμαχος γοῦν ἔφη, περὶ τῶν ἐν ᾅδου λέγων,

ἐκ τῶν ὅκου βοῦν κολλύβου πιπρήσκουσιν,

ὡς ἂν εἴποι τις τοῦ προστυχόντος, while the same suggestion recurs in Aristophanes, *Peace*, 1199 ff.

ὡς πρὸ τοῦ
οὐδεὶς ἐπρίατ' ἂν δρέπανον οὐδὲ κολλύβου,
νυνὶ δὲ πεντήκοντα δραχμῶν ἐμπολῶ,

and in Eupolis, frag. 233 Kock, quoted by the scholiast on Aristophanes, *Peace*, 1176, where κολλύβου obviously means "at a trifling cost".

Instinctively we think of our own word "mite" as affording a striking analogy.[10] Of this the Oxford *New English Dictionary* writes as follows (vi. 545):

"Originally, a Flemish copper coin of very small value; according to some early Flemish writers, worth ⅓ of a Flemish penny, though other, chiefly smaller, values are also mentioned. In Eng. used mainly as a proverbial expression for an extremely small unit of money value. In books of commercial arithmetic in 16–17th c. it commonly appears as the lowest denomination of English money of account, usually $\frac{1}{24}d$, but sometimes $\frac{1}{64}d$, and sometimes $\frac{1}{12}d$;

---

[7] Cf. the use of "barleycorn" as a measure of length, and W. Ridgeway's contention that the grain of troy weight is the equivalent of a grain of barley (*Origin of Metallic Currency*, 176 ff.).

[8] This should almost certainly be emended to ἡμιώβολον or ἡμιωβόλιον.

[9] Reinach, *op. cit.*, 145 note 2, brushes aside, a little cavalierly, the latter part of this gloss, which he regards as being either an allusion to the imperial bronze coins with the bucranium or a confusion arising out of the line of Callimachus quoted below.

[10] Reinach, *op. cit.*, 151, claims as analogous the French "liard" and "maille".

it is, however, unlikely that the word was ever in Eng. mer-
cantile use. From the 14th c. *mite* has been the usual rendering
(though the Wyclif versions have 'mynutis') of L. *minūtum*
(Vulg.), Gr. λεπτόν in Mark xii. 43, where two 'mites' are stated
to make a 'farthing' (Gr. κοδράντης, L. *quadrans*); hence the
word is now popularly taken as equivalent to 'half-farthing' . . .
A small weight; *spec.* the twentieth part of a grain troy."

Of multiples of the κόλλυβος we meet with the δικόλλυβον in
a quotation (preserved in Pollux, ix. 63) from Aristophanes,
Aeolosicon, frag. 3 διώβολον γεγένητ' ἐμοὶ δικόλλυβον,[11] and with the
τρικόλλυβον in Pollux, vi. 165 and ix. 72 ἔλεγον δέ τι καὶ τρικόλλυβον
οἱ ποιηταὶ σμικρὸν νόμισμα, and in Hesychius τρικόλ(λ)υβον· νομισμάτιόν τι.

Occasionally κόλλυβος is used, in either the singular or the plural,
to denote "small change" in general, as in Origen's phrase διδόντες
κόλλυβα τοῖς προσιοῦσιν, εὐτελῆ καὶ εὐκαταφρόνητα νομίσματα (iv. 191 B)
and in Suetonius, *Aug.* 4 " manibus collybo decoloratis ".

Into the difficult numismatic problems of the material of the
Attic κόλλυβος and of the number of κόλλυβοι composing the χαλκοῦς
(usually held to be four, though the evidence is inconclusive) I do
not propose to enter, for I have no fresh suggestions to offer. In
a well-known article Svoronos sought to identify as κόλλυβοι the
tiny bronze coins or *tesserae*, dating from the second half of the fifth
century B.C., which have been found in large numbers in Attica,
and in Attica only.[12] Reinach, on the other hand, after sum-
marizing and criticizing the views of his predecessors, concludes
that κόλλυβος was the nickname popularly given to a tiny silver
coin, which he identifies with the ἡμιτεταρτημόριον, or eighth part of

---

[11] The form δικόλλυβος, given by Liddell and Scott, is an error.
[12] See B. V. Head, *Historia Numorum*², 390f., F. Hultsch, *Metrologie*²,
227 ff., J. N. Svoronos, *Journ. Intern. d'Arch. Num.*, xiv. 123 ff., P. Gardner,
History of Ancient Coinage, 295 ff., K. Regling in Pauly–Wissowa, *R.-E.*, xi.
1099 f., *Wörterbuch der Münzkunde*, 314. Gardner says : "Mr. Svoronos main-
tains that the only bronze coin issued at Athens in the fifth century was
the κόλλυβος, a small piece introduced by Demetrius surnamed ὁ Χαλκός about
430 B.C. Such small pieces of bronze have long been known at Athens;
Mr. Svoronos publishes a long list. I am by no means convinced by his
arguments. . . . I adhere to the usual view that these pieces were not currency,
but tesserae " (p. 296 f.). In this view Th. Reinach and G. P. Oikonomos
concur (*Rev. Num.*, xxxi. 154).

an obol; this coin, he holds, was replaced by the bronze χαλκοῦς about 370 B.C.[13]

Whatever may have been the case during the period of the Peloponnesian War, when the pressure of events necessitated recourse to novel and exceptional expedients, the fact that the κόλλυβος did not enter into Athenian commercial transactions during the fourth and following centuries seems to me to be a legitimate inference from the silence alike of literature (the line of Callimachus quoted above provides no significant exception) and of the large number of inscriptions which record sums of money, always precise and frequently descending to very low denominations. Among these the χαλκοῦς repeatedly appears, either written in full or indicated by the acrophonic symbol X, but never a fraction of that coin, and thus the way was opened for the use of κόλλυβος in its secondary sense as " deduction for exchange". Especially significant is the *abacus* from Salamis, now in the Epigraphical Museum at Athens (*IG* ii². 2777), on which are engraved three series of monetary signs (not pure numbers) in descending order of value ; these begin in one case with T ⌐ᴙ (1 talent, 5,000 dr.), in the other two with X⌐ᴙ (1000 dr., 500 dr.), but in all three the final signs are ⊢ICTX (1 dr., 1 ob., ½ ob., ¼ ob., 1 chalkous), showing that no lower denomination was recognized.[14]

But we must not assume that what held good at Athens applied equally throughout the rest of the Greek world. It is true, and only natural, that in the great majority of Greek states the smallest coin which meets us in epigraphical records is the χαλκοῦς, but this rule is not without exceptions.

In *BSA* xxviii. 151 ff. (cf. 143) I gave a new and much fuller text of an inscription found in the village of Bougázi in Messenia, not far from the site of the ancient Andania, and now preserved in the Epigraphical Museum at Athens (*IG* v (i). 1532). This contains part of a list of payments, probably compulsory,[15] made by

---

[13] *Rev. Num.*, xxxi. 150 ff.

[14] For the Attic system of acrophonic numerals and money-symbols see W. Larfeld, *Handbuch d. griech. Epigraphik*, ii. 543 ff., and M. N. Tod, *BSA* xviii. 100 f., 127 ff., xxviii. 150 f., xxxvii. 237 f.

[15] See A. Wilhelm, *Jahresh.* xvii. 87 ff. Had the payments been voluntary, they would have consisted of round sums and shown a tendency towards standardization.

a large number of individuals and one community (πόλις), recorded in minas, staters, drachmas, and obols. There are signs for the half-obol (<) and quarter-obol (>) and for the χαλκοῦς (X), while in no fewer than seven cases the κόλλυβος (K) appears as the lowest denomination. From the fact that this last sign is in no case doubled I inferred (p. 157) that, in Messenia at least, the κόλλυβος was half of the χαλκοῦς, and this still seems to me to be probable, though not proved.

A second case has just come to my notice, where the evidence is much slighter, but not, I think, negligible. In the most recent issue [16] of the *BCH* (lxvi–lxvii, 84 ff.) J. Bousquet publishes a number of new fragments of the Delphian accounts dating from the fourth century B.C. Among these are (pp. 119 ff.) three contiguous fragments of a slab of local limestone (Inv. 7005), discovered by P. Amandry in July, 1942, on which are engraved στοιχηδόν portions of two columns recording payments of rent. The editor has restored the text on the basis of the extant portions of similar lists collected and edited, under the title " Locations et fermages des biens confisqués ", by E. Bourguet in *Fouilles de Delphes*, iii (5), pp. 65 ff., Nos. 15–18. The entries in the new fragments tally exactly, save for certain trifling differences in the amounts of the "baux primitifs" when compared with the previous lists, which are all uniform : of these divergences the editor has no explanation to suggest (p. 122). Among the payments registered in column I are three of special interest, namely

l. 4   [στατῆρας ἑκατὸν δύο ὀβολοὺς πέ]ντε ⲤΓ,

l. 8   [στατῆρας τεσσαράκοντα δύο] ὀβολὸν Χ,

l. 10 [στατῆρας ὀκτὼ ὀβολο]ὺς δύο ΧK.

We have here, though the editor does not call attention to it, by far the earliest appearance at Delphi of acrophonic monetary symbols. I have commented elsewhere [17] upon the surprising rarity of such symbols in Delphian inscriptions. Apart from a few sporadic examples of the expression by such means of the ransom-prices of freedmen, found in manumission-records of the second and first centuries B.C., I have discovered only one Delphian document,

[16] This is the volume for 1942–3, but it was published in 1944 and did not become accessible in Oxford until early in 1946.

[17] *BSA* xviii. 110 f., xxxvii. 245 ff.

an account of work carried out in the gymnasium, stadium, and hippodrome in 258 B.C., in which such signs are used, both for pure numbers and for money values,[18] of which the lower denominations are ⊢Ι⊂ΤΧ. No such signs occur in any of the many and extensive financial records of the fourth century collected in *Fouilles de Delphes*, iii (5). Bousquet's new fragment warns us that we should be mistaken if we concluded from the *argumentum ex silentio* that no such numeral system was known at Delphi. Its use in this case —only, be it noted, to a minimum extent—is clearly due to the engraver's determination not to use more than two lines, narrowed by the exigencies of the columnar arrangement, for any single item in his list;[19] he has recourse to other means of abbreviation also, as for example the omission, in ll. 6, 18, of the last letters of τέτορας. Bousquet recognized the Χ of l. 8 as representing the χαλκοῦς, but regarded the Χк of l. 10 as merely a variant of it.[20] I cannot share this view, but interpret the к as standing for a κόλλυβος and so indicating the circulation at Delphi of a fraction of the χαλκοῦς—what fraction the evidence does not enable us to determine.

Still less happy, in my judgement, is Bousquet's treatment of the signs ⊂Γ in l. 4, of which he writes, "le second signe doit équivaloir à 5 ; le premier, peu net, a l'air d'être le signe courant de la demi-obole, mais on s'explique mal l'expression 'cinq demi-oboles', venant après cinq oboles (ou 5 drachmes)".[21] The first sign is indeed that which at Delphi (see above) and in some other Greek states (Athens, Epidaurus, Thyrrheum, Delos, Amorgos, Eretria, Teos) represents the half-obol, the second must stand for 5 χαλκοῖ. It is possible that a closer examination might discover a small Χ in the heart of the Γ, but this need not be assumed ; the descending order of value in which acrophonic symbols are invariably arranged shows that Γ must represent a sum smaller than

[18] *Ibid.* xviii. 111 and fig. 2 (p. 107).
[19] For the same reason of spatial economy we also frequently, in making out a cheque, write the pounds in letters, the shillings and pence in figures.
[20] On p. 121 he speaks of "le signe Χ ou Χк pour le chalque".
[21] The addition of "ou 5 drachmes" is unfortunate, for it overlooks the fact that in these rent-lists the reckoning is in staters, so that the drachma, if it occurs at all, must be in the singular : 5 dr. would be expressed as 2 st. 1 dr.

C, its form proves that it represents five units of some denomination, which here can only be the χαλκοῦς. Since, then, the obol at Delphi consisted of twelve χαλκοῖ, CΓ must stand for 6 + 5, i.e. 11, χαλκοῖ. Once at least we find in Delphian accounts the words χαλκοῖ ἕνδεκα written out in full (*Fouilles de Delphes*, iii (5), 9 i 2), and in the Epidaurian temple-accounts of the fourth century we find Γ standing for 5 ch. (*IG* iv² (1). 102. 172, 178, 189, 292) and <Γ for 11 ch. (*ibid.* 221), if, as I believe, the Epidaurian obol also contained 12 χαλκοῖ.[22]

But we have here passed from the study of the κόλλυβος to that of the χαλκοῦς, the consideration of which must be left to a further note.   MARCUS N. TOD.

---

[22] In *BSA* xxxvii. 243, fig. 1 the numbers 102 and 103 should be transposed.

EPIGRAPHICAL NOTES ON GREEK COINAGE[1]
II. ΧΑΛΚΟΥΣ

IF, as I tried to show in my previous note (*Num. Chron.* 1945, 108–116), Greek inscriptions make some contribution to the study of the κόλλυβος, their contribution is more varied and more valuable when we turn to the χαλκοῦς. I repeat at the outset, though it may well be that the contents of this note will render the avowal superfluous, that I make no claim to be a numismatist or a metrologist, but approach the subject solely from the standpoint of Greek epigraphy.[2] My impression that students of antiquity are tempted in this age of specialization to work too much in watertight compartments is confirmed by the discovery that of the articles in *RE* on Chalkus (Kubitschek), Dichalkon (Hultsch), Trichalkon (Schwabacher), and Tetrachalkon (Regling) three make no reference at all to inscriptions, while Hultsch confines himself to the remark that "das *trichalcon* bei Vitruv ist das Viertel des aeginaeischen Obolos, auf dessen Duodecimalteilung aus boiotischen und phokischen Inschriften zu schliessen ist (Hultsch *Jahrb. f. class. Philol.* 1892, 24 f.)." Nor do I find a single allusion to any inscription in the articles on these same four words contributed by that distinguished numismatist K. Regling to F. von Schrötter's *Wörterbuch der Münzkunde*.

We may start with LS, where we read "χαλκοῦς, ὁ, *copper coin* used at Athens, ⅛ of an obol, Ar. *Ec.* 815, 818, D. 42. 22, Alex. 15. 2, Philem. 64, 74, Cerc. 17. 41, Plu. 2. 665 b, etc. : in pl., *money*, *PCair. Zen.* 519 (iii B.C.), etc." This omits all reference to χαλκοῦς as a value (see below) and as a weight, uses "copper" where "bronze" would be more exact, leaves the impression that the χαλκοῦς is specifically Attic, fails to mention that in many states

---

[1] Since the following notes are mainly linguistic and epigraphical, I shall have frequent occasion to refer to Liddell and Scott's *Greek-English Lexicon* (new edition, 1925–40), which I denote by LS ; for economy of space I adopt in my references to periodicals and to epigraphical and papyrological publications the abbreviations used in that work (Introduction, pp. xli–xlvi). For Pauly-Wissowa-Kroll, *Realencyclopädie der classischen Altertumswissenschaft*, I use the initials *RE*.

[2] For the numismatic approach see E. Babelon, *Traité des monnaies grecques et romaines*, i. 460 ff. ; for the metrological, F. Hultsch, *Metrol. Scriptores*, ii. 224 f., *Griechische und römische Metrologie*[2], 133 f., 227 ff., 337 ff.

the χαλκοῦς was, as we shall see, $\frac{1}{12}$ of an obol, and in some perhaps a different fraction, and contains no epigraphical reference. Moreover, the same lexicon under the letter X informs us that "in Inscrr., X stands for χίλιοι, αι, α, = 1,000", passing over in silence its use as the acrophonic sign for χαλκοῦς.

Χαλκοῦς is the Attic contraction for χάλκεος. In Boeotian dialect inscriptions (IG vii. 2420, 3193) the form χάλκιος is used, with an accusative plural χαλκίως; at Epidaurus the uncontracted χάλκεος occurs throughout the fourth-century building-records (IG iv² (1) 103, 106, 110), and χάλκεος is also found at Delphi in some of the fourth-century financial documents (Delph. iii (5) 15 passim, 80. 14, 85. 19), though it was soon superseded by the contracted Attic χαλκοῦς (ibid. 16, 17, 18, 50 passim, etc.) even in dialect inscriptions; thus we find the phrase χαλκοῖ τέτορες (ibid. 23 ii 34, 28. 8, 44. 2).

The word is always used in the masculine, though we might have expected it to be in the neuter, with νόμισμα understood.[3] What noun we must supply is uncertain. W. Kubitschek suggests (RE iii. 2098) that, since the χαλκοῦς is a fraction of the obol, ὀβολός should be supplied rather than στατήρ, but this argument is unconvincing since it leaves out of account the parallel formations ἀργυροῦς and χρυσοῦς, where the word understood is in all probability στατήρ.[4] Similarly formed is the Byzantine coin-name σιδάρεος, of which Pollux writes (ix. 78) Βυζαντίων γε μὴν σιδήρῳ νομιζόντων ἦν οὕτω καλούμενος σιδάρεος νόμισμά τι λεπτόν, ὥστε ἀντὶ τοῦ "πρίω μοι τριῶν χαλκῶν" λέγειν "πρίω μοι τριῶν σιδαρέων".[5] He

---

[3] In SIG 530. 6 (Dyme, 3rd cent. B.C.) [νό]μισμα ἔκοπτον χάλ[κεον] refers to the coining of bronze money in general, and OGI 339. 44 (Sestus, 2nd cent. B.C.) νομίσματι χαλκίνωι χρῆσθαι ἰδίωι relates to the use of a bronze currency. Similarly OGI 484. 40 f. (Pergamum, 2nd cent. A.D.) τῇ τοῦ ἀργυροῦ νομίσ[μα]|τος δόσει is used of a silver coinage; cf. OGI 515. 28, 59.

[4] Cf. OGI 6. 27 (Scepsis, about 311 B.C.) [ἀπὸ στατήρ]ων χρυσῶν ἑκατόν, followed in l. 29 by χρυσοῖ[ς πεν]τήκοντα, and Hsch. ἄργυρος· ὁ στατήρ. We may note the remark of Pollux, ix. 59 εἰ μὲν χρυσοῦς εἴποις, προσυπακούεται ὁ στατήρ, εἰ δὲ στατήρ, οὐ πάντως ὁ χρυσοῦς.

[5] Hesychius has a puzzling entry σιδάριος· χαλκεύς. In his larger edition (Jena, 1861) M. Schmidt retained this, the reading of the codex, but in his commentary asked "Nonne σιδαρεύς vel aeolice σιδάριος· χαλκοῦς (Theocr. 29, 24)?" In his editio minor² (Jena, 1867) he wrote in the text σιδάριος (Theocr. xxix 24)· χαλκοῦς. I gravely doubt whether the lexicographer had the Theocritean passage in mind, and am inclined to wonder whether he wrote σιδάρεος· χαλκοῦς with reference to the Byzantine coinage described in his immediately preceding gloss.

proceeds to quote two lines of Strattis, *Myrmidones*, to which LS adds Aristophanes, *Clouds*, 248 f., τῷ γὰρ ὄμνυτ'; ἢ | σιδαρέοισιν ὥσπερ ἐν Βυζαντίῳ; and Plato Comicus, 96. We may compare also Hesychius' entry *s.v.* σιδάρεοι θεοί.

Χαλκίον was in popular use to denote a bronze coin,[6] but was not the official name of any specific denomination (cf. Pollux, ix. 90 ff., who quotes Aristophanes, *Frogs*, 721 ff., and Eubulus, fr. 83); thus we colloquially refer to any "copper" coin as "a copper". The use of the diminutive may have been due, at least in part, to the smallness of the sums paid in bronze, though the same derogatory sense does not seem to attach to ἀργύριον or χρυσίον, but had to be imparted by the double diminutive forms, as in Isocrates, xiii. 4 ἀργυρίδιον καὶ χρυσίδιον τὸν πλοῦτον ἀποκαλοῦντες. Χαλκός, which primarily means "copper" or "bronze", is also used of objects made of this metal and sometimes collectively of copper money or of money in general, irrespective of its material (see references in LS). Thus Pollux says (ix. 92) ἡ δὲ τῶν πολλῶν καὶ ἰδιωτῶν χρῆσις τὸν χαλκὸν τὸ ἀργύριον λέγει, οἷον "οὐκ ἔχω χαλκόν" καὶ "ὀφείλω χαλκόν", for which latter phrase he quotes Epicharmus, *Persae*. This same meaning of "money" occasionally attaches to χαλκοῖ, as in *SIG* 631. 12 (Delphi, second century B.C.) ἀπὸ τῶν χαλκῶν τῶν καταλιμπάνει, *IG* xiv. 759. 15 (Naples) τοὺς δὲ χαλκοῦς[7] οἱ δεδανεισμένοι καταφερέτωσαν, and Herondas, vii. 49 f. ἀλλ' οὐ λόγων γάρ, φασίν, ἡ ἀγορὴ δεῖται, χαλκῶν δέ.

With fractions of the χαλκοῦς I have already dealt in my note on the κόλλυβος, and here I need only add that the word ἡμίχαλκον does not, so far as I know, occur. I now turn to the various multiples of the χαλκοῦς.

Δίχαλκον is thus defined in LS: "*double chalcus, a copper coin, = ¼ of an obol, AP* 11. 165 (Lucill.), Poll. 9. 65; *as a weight (variously expld.), Dsc. 4. 150, etc.*" This is not wholly satis-

---

[6] Cf. Hsch. χαλκίον· τὸν χαλκοῦν. It was only by a *lapsus calami* that Hultsch wrote "τὰ πονηρὰ χαλκία, nummi aurei (*sic*) Atheniensium" (*Metrol. Script.* ii. 224).

[7] In *GDI* 5272. 15 and in the Index (p. 992) Bechtel wrongly wrote τοὺς χαλκούς. Similarly Kolbe wrote χαλκοί throughout *IG* v (1) 1433 and in the Index (p. 344), though he correctly wrote χαλκοῖ in the commentary. More serious is Paton's inadvertence in indexing the phrase ἀπὸ χρυσῶν δισχιλίων in *IG* xii (2) 58 *b* 28 under χρυσά (p. 150).

factory, for (1) it distinguishes only two meanings of the word, coin and weight, and omits all reference to the third, value or sum of money; (2) it uses the term "copper" where "bronze" would be preferable; (3) it suggests that the δίχαλκον is everywhere, as it is in Attica and some other states, a quarter of an obol, overlooking those regions in which the obol comprised twelve, or possibly more, χαλκοῖ, and (4) of the authors cited Lucillius and Dioscorides belong to the first, Pollux to the second, century of our era. The word can, in fact, be traced back to the fourth century B.C., for there can be little doubt that the legend ΔΙΧΑΛΚΙΗ on the reverse of a fourth-century bronze coin of Apollonia Pontica, now in the British Museum (Head, *Hist. Num.*² 277), must be read as δίχαλκ(ον) ΙΗ.[8] For the third century B.C. there is not only the indirect evidence of the adjective διχαλκιαῖος, used in a papyrus of about 260 B.C. (*PCair. Zen.* 59019. 5, cited in the addenda to LS), but the occurrence of the word itself in a tax-receipt from Diospolis Magna, dated 209 B.C. (*Sammelb.* 5729. 9 τὸ παρ' ἀμφοτέρων τέλος ὀκτὼ δυοβόλους δίχαλκον). It is found on a Theban ostrakon now in Leningrad, probably dating from the reign of Marcus Aurelius (*Arch. Pap.* v. 173, No. 10 δραχμαὶ (sic) μίαν ὀβολοὶ δύο ἥμισυ δίχαλκον), on ten ostraka included in U. Wilcken's *Griechische Ostraka* (see the Index, ii, p. 489) and in Vitruvius iii. 1. 7 *quadrantesque obolorum, quae alii dichalca, nonnulli trichalca dicunt*. It is also written out in full, ΔΙΧΑΛΚΟΝ, on the reverse of certain bronze coins of Chios dating from the Imperial period (Head, *Hist. Num.*² 601, *B.M. Cat. Coins: Ionia*, 341). Lastly, it appears in Hesychius *s.v.* ταρτημόριον, in Suidas *s.v.* τεταρτημόριον, and in Photius and the *Etymologicum Magnum s.v.* ταρτημόριον.

Τρίχαλκον is defined in LS as "*a coin worth three χαλκοῖ*", and references are given to Theophrastus, *Characters*, 10. 6, *IG* iv² (1) 109 iii 128 (an Epidaurian building-inscription of the third century B.C.), *IG* v (1) 1433. 33 (a Messenian document, apparently recording

---

[8] Cf. M. N. Tod, *BSA* xxviii. 150, F. Bechtel, *GDI* 5541 (2). The letters ΙΗ, also found on coins of Apollonia now in Berlin and at Gotha, may be the abbreviation of a magistrate's name, e.g. Ἰητραγόρης, or it may, as Bechtel suggested, represent the ἐπίκλησις of the principal god of the city, Ἀπόλλων ἰητρός (cf. the legend Ἀπόλλωνος ἰατροῦ on the reverse of an Apollonian bronze coin of the third or a later century, Head, *Hist. Num.*² 278). Regling mistakenly regards διχαλκίη as a variant of δίχαλκον (*Wörterbuch der Münzkunde, s.v.*).

sums payable to the Romans as tribute), and Vitruvius iii. 1. 7
(quoted above). To these we may add *IG* iv² (1) 109 iii 140
δρα[χμ]ᾶν δύο τριχάλκου, 116. 15 πέντε ὀβολῶν τριχάλκου, and the
legend ΤΡΙΧΑΛΚΟΝ on the obverse of an Imperial bronze coin of
Chios (Head, *Hist. Num.*² 601, *B.M. Cat. Coins: Ionia*, 340). The
word is also used to denote a weight, not a sum of money, in
P. Wolters–G. Bruns, *Das Kabirenheiligtum bei Theben*, i. 21, No. 2,
l. 9 ὁλκὰ δύ' ὀβολοὶ τρίχαλκο[ν], an inscription of about 200 B.C.,
which is a revised edition of a text published by E. Szanto, *Ath.
Mitt.* xv. 379 ff., by W. Dittenberger, *IG* vii. 2420, and by C. Michel,
Recueil, 828 (where other bibliographical references will be found).
Szanto read δυοβολοὶ τριχαλκίο[ν], Dittenberger δύ' ὀβολοὶ τρῖ⟨ς⟩
χάλκιοι, and Michel δύ' ὀβολοὶ τριχαλκίο[ν]. In his commentary
Wolters remarks (*loc. cit.* p. 22) that "the earlier reading τριχαλκίον
must be abandoned. On the squeeze I now believe that I see
ΤΡΙΧΑΛΚΟΝ. Karo, who together with Messrs. Keramopullos and
Bizard examined the stone, sees "ΤΡΙΧΑΛΚΟ, then perhaps a
further stroke, certainly not ΚΙΟΝ or ΚΟΝ". As Hultsch notes,
the τρίχαλκον is not a *coin*, for the gold is weighed according to the
Attic *weight* (*B.C.H.* 1882, 139 f.). The Attic obol weighs 0·73 gr.;
the chalcus-weight is thus 0·09 gr. and the τρίχαλκον 0·27 gr."
Wolters also calls attention to the fact that "the indication of
weight in l. 9 is scratched in an unsteady hand, that is to say, it
was not entered by the stonemason, but only after the weight had
been ascertained by an official". A Phocian bronze coin issued
during the Third Sacred War, about 357–346 B.C., bears on the
reverse, surrounded by a laurel wreath, the sign Τ (Head, *Hist.
Num.*² 339, *B.M. Cat. Coins: Central Greece*, xxvii f., 22), which the
numismatists with some hesitation interpret as τρίχαλκον, regarding
this as more probable than τριτεταρτημόριον (K. Regling in *Wörterbuch der Münzkunde*, 702, *s.v.* Trichalkon, W. Schwabacher in *RE*
vii A 84). To me it seems more likely that, if the coin is indeed a
τρίχαλκον, the Τ stands for (τε)ταρτημόριον, which, in a state where
1 obol = 12 χαλκοῖ, is equivalent to τρίχαλκον. Otherwise, it may
stand for τριτημόριον (= 4 ch.), but that it should represent τριτεταρτημόριον (= 9 ch.) is highly improbable.

Τετράχαλκον does not appear at all in LS. The word is, however,
found on the reverse of Imperial bronze coins of Chios (Head,

Hist. Num.[2] 601, *B.M. Cat. Coins: Ionia*, 340) and in two entries of Hesychius, *s.v.* ἵππορ (cod. ἱπποπορ)· τόν τε ἵππον, καὶ τὸν τετρά- χαλκον. . . . Λάκωνες (where I suggest that we should read τὸ τετράχαλκον), and *s.v.* πέλανορ· τὸ τετράχαλκον. Λάκωνες. The rarity of the word may be explained, at least in part, by the fact that in all states of the Greek world, including Attica, where the obol comprised eight χαλκοῖ the word ἡμιωβέλιον, in one of its various forms, was used in preference to τετράχαλκον.[9]

Πεντέχαλκον occurs in LS, with the definition "*piece of five χαλκοῖ*", as used by the comic poet Aristophon, 2. The passage in question is quoted by Pollux (ix. 70) καὶ πεντέχαλκον δὲ τοὺς πέντε χαλκοῦς ὠνομασμένους εὕρομεν ἐν τοῖς Ἀριστοφῶντος Διδύμοις ἢ Πυραύνῳ·

ἔπειθ' ἡπάτια καὶ νῆστίν τινα

προσέθηκεν, οἶμαι, πεντέχαλκον προσλαβών.

See also Photius *s.v.* πεντέπηχυ.

Ἑξάχαλκον presents a more difficult problem. In LS we read "ἑξάχαλκος [ᾰ], ὁ, *coin of the value of six χαλκοῖ*, *IG* 5 (1) 1433. 29 (Messene)". This inscription, cited above for τρίχαλκον, expresses a certain sum of money as χίλια διακόσια τεσσαράκοντα τάλαντα, τέσ- σαρες μναῖ, τριάκοντα στατῆρες, δύ' ὀβολοί, ἑξάχαλκοι (*sic*). In ten out of the other eleven places in this inscription where χαλκοῖ are men- tioned the entry takes the form δέκα χαλκοῖ (ll. 7, 10, 21), ἐννέα χαλκοῖ (l. 35), ἓξ χαλκοῖ (ll. 36, 37, 38, 40 *a*, 42, 43); only once (l. 33) does the form τρίχαλκον occur. I fully acknowledge that the Greeks were not always rigidly consistent in their word-formations, yet I cannot here accept the masculine form ἑξάχαλκος, especially as the stone shows the meaningless plural ἑξάχαλκοι. I therefore suggest that either (1) the stonemason, or whatever official prepared the drawings on which the engraver based his work, intended to write ΕΞΑΧΑΛΚΟΝ (cf. ΤΡΙΧΑΛΚΟΝ in l. 33), but omitted to complete the final letter, or, preferably, (2) that he intended to write ΕΞΑΛΚΟΙ, as in the six other places noted above, but inserted a redundant Α, perhaps misled by his knowledge of the existence of a form ἑξάχαλκον. In view of the excellent preservation of the stone's surface and of Kolbe's skill as a copyist, I do not suggest that a Ν on the stone has been misread as Ι. In the 'Addenda et

---

[9] Cf. Hsch. τετρᾶντα· τετράγωνόν τι σχῆμα. δηλοῖ δὲ καὶ τοὺς τέσσαρας χαλκοῦς. For similar Sicilian names see Poll. ix. 80 f., quoted in footnote 14.

Corrigenda' (p. 311) Kolbe states that the true reading of *IG* v (1) 1433. 29 is δέκα χαλκοῖ. This confirms my rejection of ἐξάχαλκοι, but renders my argument unnecessary. I have corrected accordingly the references to this inscription on pp. 54, 57.

'Επτάχαλκον. Although it is irrelevant to our present inquiry, I note in passing the reference to τὴν περὶ τὸ 'Επτάχαλκον ἔφοδον found in Plutarch's account of Sulla's siege of Athens (*Sulla*, 14). What is the precise meaning of the word and the exact location of the place denoted by it we cannot determine; for the latter question see W. Judeich, *Topographie von Athen*², 368.

Δεκάχαλκον appears in LS as "*coin worth ten* χαλκοῖ, = Lat. *denarius* (*worth ten asses*), Plu. *Cam.* 13", where we read ἀσσάριον γὰρ ἦν τὸ ἀργύριον, καὶ τὸ δεκάχαλκον οὕτως ἐκαλεῖτο δηνάριον.

That the foregoing list of references is complete I do not for a moment claim, but it must be admitted that it is surprisingly short. A twofold explanation of this fact is not, I think, far to seek. In the first place, multiples of the χαλκοῦς can be, and very often are, expressed as fractions of the next higher denomination, the obol. Not only does ἡμιωβέλιον tend, as I have suggested above, to supersede τετράχαλκον, or, in other states, ἑξάχαλκον, but other multiples of the χαλκοῦς are replaced by the fractions τριτημόριον and (τε)ταρτημόριον. These words I hope to discuss in a subsequent note on the obol. Secondly, it must be borne in mind that, strictly speaking, δίχαλκον, τρίχαλκον, and the rest denote coins and not values or sums of money as such. The distinction between the two closely related meanings is often overlooked, both in antiquity and at the present time; otherwise the foregoing list would have been considerably shorter than it is. If, to give a very simple illustration, I say "I promise to give you a shilling", the word "shilling" may denote a coin of that specific denomination, or it may refer to a certain worth or value expressed in terms of money. If it bears the former meaning, my promise can be redeemed only by the payment of one silver coin; if the latter, it can be equally fulfilled by the payment of two silver sixpences or of four silver or nickel threepenny-pieces or of twelve "copper" pennies. Now it is in the latter rather than in the former sense that money values are, in the great majority of cases, recorded in inscriptions, and in consequence we should expect to find, and we actually do find, that the occurrences

of χαλκοῖ preceded or followed by a numeral far outnumber those
of a compound of the type δίχαλκον. For example, in the Messenian
inscription already cited, *IG* v (1) 1433, τρίχαλκον is used only once,
but δέκα, ἐννέα, or ἐξ χαλκοῖ occur eleven times.

I now come to a brief recapitulation of the evidence for the
circulation of the χαλκοῦς provided by the appearance in Greek
inscriptions of some abbreviation of, or symbol for, that word. In
three successive articles, *BSA* xviii. 98 ff., xxviii. 141 ff., xxxvii.
236 ff., I collected and discussed the materials, so far as known to
me, relative to the employment in the Greek world of the acrophonic system of numeral notation and its application to the representation of money, weights, and measures, and I added (xxxvii.
258) an alphabetical list of the places where the use of such a
system is attested. We may note in the present connexion that
in a very large proportion of the examples there examined the
abbreviation or symbol indicates a sum of money and not a pure
number.

As was to be expected in an acrophonic system, the χαλκοῦς is
normally represented by its initial letter X. This was, it is true,
also used to represent 1,000 or 1,000 drachmas (this lies, I suppose,
at the basis of Hesychius' curious entry χεῖ· ἐπὶ τῶν χιλίων δραχμῶν
τοῦτο ἐχάραττον), but no actual ambiguity was caused, since the
context or the order in which the sign appeared in a money-complex
sufficiently indicated what value the X represented in any given
case. This sign is found in inscriptions of Attica (*BSA* xviii. 101,
xxxvii. 237), Andania (xxviii. 143, 156), Tegea (xviii. 105 f.), Oropus
(xxviii. 143), Thespiae (xxxvii. 244), Acraephia (xxxvii. 245), Delphi
(xviii. 107, 111; cf. *Num. Chron.* 1945, 114 ff.), Thyrrheum in Acarnania (xxviii. 144 f.), Delos (xviii. 116), Eretria (xxviii. 145), and
perhaps also Erythrae in Ionia (xxviii. 147 f.). Various other
symbols also are employed to denote the χαλκοῦς, O at Troezen
(xviii. 105), C at Corcyra (xviii. 112 f.), · at Chalcedon (xviii. 120),
Σ or Σ at Epidaurus (xxxvii. 239 ff.), and possibly also at Nemea
(xviii. 103) and at Pergamum (xviii. 120), / or \, rarely —, and at
least once | at Delos (xviii. 116, xxxvii. 250), and perhaps ' at
Thebes (xxxvii. 245). To the evidence discussed in those articles
I can now add the | which occurs as the equivalent of the χαλκοῦς
in an inscription, already cited (above, p. 51), from the sanctuary

of the Cabiri near Thebes, where Wolters's new edition of *IG* vii. 2420 gives in l. 26 τρῖς ὀβολοὶ ΙΙ, which can hardly mean anything other than 3 obols 2 χαλκοῖ. I repeat what I said in my note on the κόλλυβος (*Num. Chron.* 1945, 114 ff.), that the ΧΚ of a fourth-century Delphian inscription (*BCH* lxvi–vii. 119 i 9/10; cf. 120 ii 10/11) cannot stand, as the editor suggests, for χ(αλ)κ(οῦς), but must represent one χαλκοῦς and one κόλλυβος. Of signs denoting 5 χαλκοῖ we find ⋈ on an Argive coin (*BSA* xviii. 125; see below, note 11), Γ, or possibly ⋈, at Delphi (*Num. Chron. loc. cit.*), Γ at Epidaurus (*BSA* xxxvii. 240), and ΓΧ at Acraephia (*BSA* xxxvii. 245), if Feyel's interpretation is correct. For Τ possibly representing τρίχαλκον see above, p. 51.

I am not qualified to discuss the frequent appearances of χαλκοῖ in papyri and ostraka, where, as we have already seen (p. 50), the word δίχαλκον also occurs, but not, so far as I know, any other compound of this type. I call attention in passing, however, to the signs used to denote the obol and its fractions, of which fac-similes will be found in the relevant index to vol. i of the *Berliner Griechische Urkunden*. The obol is represented by a horizontal line, with or without a dot under its middle point, the χαλκοῦς by a cursive χ, sometimes differentiated by a flourish, frequently having a small α directly above it or above to the right (in the position of an algebraical index), 2 χαλκοῖ by a Χ with a small β above to the right or a small o attached to or standing above the letter, 3 χαλκοῖ by a Χ with a small γ above on the right, 4 χαλκοῖ by the half-sign, C, followed by a straight stroke slanting upwards, 5, 6, and 7 χαλκοῖ by C followed by Χ with α, β, γ respectively above it or to the right. Here we have an interesting combination of the acrophonic element (Χ) with the purely conventional (—, C) and the use of numerals of the "alphabetic" type (α, β, γ).

Finally, we must ask what help, if any, inscriptions afford in determining the number of χαλκοῖ contained in the obol in various Greek states.

In the case of ATTICA epigraphical help is superfluous, for we have the express assertions of the lexicographers to answer the question, even if we set aside for the moment the puzzling problem of the τριτημόριον and the (τε)ταρτημόριον. Thus Pollux says in ix. 65 ὁ μέντοι ὀβολὸς ὀκτὼ χαλκοῦς εἶχεν ... οἱ δὲ τέτταρες χαλκο

ἡμιωβόλιον κτλ., in ix. 66 τεττάρων γὰρ καὶ εἴκοσι χαλκῶν ὄντων ἐν τῷ
τριωβόλῳ κτλ., and in ix. 67 ὅτι δὲ οἱ τέτταρες χαλκοῖ ἡμιωβόλιόν εἰσιν,
ἐν τῷ αὐτῷ δράματι Φιλήμονος ἔστιν·
> ὀβολοῦ τὸ πρῶτον ἡμῖν ἐνέχεει,
> καὶ τεττάρων χαλκῶν μετὰ ταῦτα. καὶ μάλα
> τρί᾽ ἡμιωβόλι᾽ ἐστί·

Suidas, too, defines τεταρτημόριον as δίχαλκον. ὁ γὰρ χαλκοῦς ὄγδοον
τοῦ ὀβολοῦ, and again as τὸ τέταρτον μέρος τοῦ ὀβολοῦ· τουτέστι χαλκοῖ
δύο, a definition which recurs in the *Etymologicum Magnum* with
the addition ὁ γὰρ ὀβολὸς ὀκτὼ χαλκοῦς ἔχει, while the same lexicon
defines ταρτημόριον as δίχαλκον· ὁ γὰρ χαλκοῦς ὄγδοον τοῦ ὀβολοῦ.[10]

For other states, however, we possess no such literary evidence,
and for some of them inscriptions give valuable information.

For EPIDAURUS we have abundant materials in the extensive
building-records which have come to light in the Epidaurian
Asclepieum, but these are not altogether easy to interpret. In my
first discussion of the problem (*BSA* xviii. 103 ff.) I followed M.
Fraenkel, who had edited the relevant documents in *IG* iv, in
taking ⊆ to represent two χαλκοῖ and X to denote a single χαλκοῦς,
one-eighteenth of an obol. In 1929 the texts in question were
republished in *IG* iv²(1) 102 ff. by F. Hiller von Gaertringen, who
at first (p. 43) accepted Fraenkel's interpretation of the signs used
to indicate money-values, but later (p. 70), realizing the difficulties
involved, substituted a new scheme of his own, in which the obol
consisted of 24 χαλκοῖ. On the basis of the revised texts I re-
examined the whole question (*BSA* xxxvii. 238 ff.) and came to
the conclusion that both Fraenkel and Hiller were at fault, that
Σ (or Σ) and X both represent the χαλκοῦς, the former sign only
being used in *IG* iv²(1) 102, 103 and 104, the latter only in iv²(1)

[10] Other evidence might have been cited, including Hsch. *s.vv.* ταρτημόριον,
τεταρτημόριον, Photius *s.vv.* ταρτημόριον, τεταρτημόριον, Harpocration *s.vv.* τεταρτημόριον, τριτημόριον. Suidas *s.v.* τάλαντον has the curious statement ὁ δὲ
χαλκοῦς λεπτῶν ζ′ (= 7), and Photius and Suidas have ὀβολός· ὁ τόκος· εἶδος
νομίσματος· ὀβολὸς δὲ παρ᾽ Ἀθηναίοις ἕξ ἐστι χαλκῶν, ὁ δὲ χαλκοῦς λεπτῶν ἑπτά. Hultsch
writes (*RE* v. 357) "ausserdem gab es χαλκοῖ als Achtel oder Sechstel, nach
minder zuverlässigen Quellen auch als Viertel oder Drittel des Obolos (s. die
Nachweise Metrol. script. II 224 f., 234)", but for an obol of less than 8
χαλκοῖ I can find no epigraphical confirmation. For the Attic bronze coinage
see P. Gardner, *History of Ancient Coinage*, 295 ff., Head, *Hist. Num.*² 388 ff.,
B.M. Cat. Coins: Attica, xxviii ff.

105 ff. If this view is right, there is no difficulty in regarding the obol as containing 12 χαλκοῖ, a number antecedently much more probable than 18 or 24. Moreover, if my interpretation is correct, we find examples in the extant records of all the successive numbers of χαλκοῖ from 1 to 11 inclusive, but none of any higher number (*BSA* xxxvii. 240). A further argument, which I did not there use, may be drawn from the fact that among the many sums written out in full in the Epidaurian records we find τριχάλκου (109 iii 128, 140; 116. 15), [τριῶν χαλκέων] (110 *A* 21), χαλκέων πέντε (106 i 95, 97), ἐννέα χαλκέων (110 *A* 38. 45), δέκα χαλκέ ων] (106 i 86), [χαλ]κ[έ ων [ἔ]νδεκα (103. 310 ; cf. Add. p. 144), but no higher number of χαλκοῖ. The striking absence of ἐξ χαλκέων is fully explained by the frequent appearances of ἡμιωβελίου.[11]

For MESSENE we rely upon the evidence supplied by *IG* v (1) 1433, but this, though isolated, is sufficient for our present purpose. As we have already seen (p. 52 f.), we find in that inscription τρίχαλκον, six examples of ἐξ χαλκοῖ, one of ἐννέα χαλκοῖ, and four of δέκα χαλκοῖ. Here also we may, I think, confidently conclude that the obol contained 12 χαλκοῖ, and that, for some unascertainable reason, ἐξ χαλκοῖ was preferred to ἡμιωβέλιον (which occurs only in l. 1) to express the half-obol.

For ANDANIA we depend wholly upon the document (*IG* v (1) 1532) revised by me in *BSA* xxviii. 151 ff., for the reference to two χαλκοῖ in the famous mystery-inscription (*IG* v (1) 1390. 107) does not help us. My own conclusion, based upon the appearance in two places (col. i, ll. 6, 12) of XXX despite the fact that special symbols, < and >, are used in the inscription for ½-obol and ¼-obol respectively, was that "it would seem probable that the Messenian χαλκοῦς was $\frac{1}{16}$- rather than $\frac{1}{12}$- or $\frac{1}{8}$-obol" (p. 156). I now prefer to assign 12 χαλκοῖ to the obol here, and to regard the use side by side

---

[11] In the *Abhandlungen der K. Bayerischen Akademie der Wissenschaften*, xviii. 533 f., No. 16 (Munich, 1890), F. Imhoof-Blumer published a silver coin of Argos bearing on the reverse the symbol ꟼ, which he interpreted as πεντέχαλκον. On this basis he concluded that at Argos 16, or possibly even 20, χαλκοῖ went to the obol, and added in a footnote " Brandis (Münz-, Mass- und Gewichtswesen in Vorderasien, S. 293) vermuthet, dass der aigin. Obolos zu 30 Chalkus normirt gewesen sei ". I am not convinced, but, since the arguments used are purely numismatic and inscriptions throw no light upon the question, I leave it to those who are competent to pronounce judgement.

of XXX and > with the same value, 3 χαλκοῖ, as merely an example
of the occasional inconsistency of Greek engravers, like the simul-
taneous use of ἐξ χαλκοῖ and ἡμιωβέλιον in the Messenian record
already considered. If my present interpretation is correct, we
have in the inscription before us examples of 1, 2, 3, 5, 6, 7, 10,
and 11 χαλκοῖ, occasionally with the addition of a κόλλυβος.

In the fourth-century financial record from TEGEA, *IG* v (2) 6,
I represents the obol, E the half-obol, T the quarter-obol, and X the
χαλκοῦς. The duplication of X in ll. 59, 73, 84, 102, and 110 proves
that the obol contained more than 8 χαλκοῖ, since otherwise XX
would be replaced by T, while if it contained 16 or more, it is
hard to account for the absence of a triple XXX. Hence it is
almost certain that at Tegea, as in many other states, 12 χαλκοῖ =
1 obol.

A long and detailed inventory of the ἀργυρώματα τοῦ θεοῦ Ἀνφια-
[ρά]ου (*IG* vii. 3498), found in his sanctuary at OROPUS and dating
from about 150 B.C., contains a large number of weights, expressed
in alphabetic numerals and in symbols. These have been carefully
studied by B. Keil in *Hermes*, xxv. 598 ff., who came to the conclusion that simple numbers represent drachmas, S = ½ drachma =
τριώβολον, — = ⅙ drachma = ὀβολός, and X = χαλκοῦς. But here the
X is followed by a numeral indicating a particular number of
χαλκοῖ, so that, for example, XΓ = τρεῖς χαλκοῖ. The relevant weights
are ΟΧΟ (l. 4), ΞΖΧΕ (l. 26), ΝΕΧΓ (l. 58), and ΝΕΧΕ (l. 59),
representing respectively 70 dr. 9 ch., 67 dr. 6 ch., 55 dr. 3 ch.,
and 55 dr. 6 ch. Keil, who hesitated about the first example,
doubted whether at Oropus the obol contained 8 χαλκοῖ or more,
but inclined to favour "at least ten" (p. 611); if the Ο of l. 4 is
rightly read, this view is decisively confirmed, and I have little
doubt that the true number is twelve, as it is in the neighbouring
Boeotia, especially in view of the fact that all the numbers of
χαλκοῖ mentioned are multiples of three.

For BOEOTIA our available evidence is scanty, but sufficient. In
the inscription from the temple of the Cabiri near Thebes, to which
I have already referred (pp. 51, 55), we have in l. 37 πέντ' ὀβ⟨ολ⟩ὼς
ἐννία χαλκίως, which proves that here the number of χαλκοῖ in the
obol exceeded 9 and was probably 12. This is borne out by the
second-century list of the controlled prices of fish at Acraephia

discussed by M. Feyel, whose conclusions I summarize in *BSA* xxxvii. 245, as also by an inscription of Boeotian Orchomenus (*IG* vii. 3193), dated about 200 B.C., in which we find mentions of πέτταρες, πέντε (thrice), ἑπτά (thrice), ὀκτό, ἐννία (twice), δέκα (thrice), and ἕνδεκα χάλκιοι (frequently in the accusative, χαλκίως).

For DELPHI our materials are both abundant and unequivocal, pointing unmistakably to an obol of 12 χαλκοῖ. Thus in the new record discussed at the close of my note on the κόλλυβος (*Num. Chron.* 1945, 114 ff.) we have Χ, ΧΚ, χαλκοῖ δύο, χαλκοῖ ἐννῆ, and ϹΠ (i.e. 11 χαλκοῖ), while elsewhere in the same group of inscriptions we find χαλκοῖ τρεῖς and δραχμὰς τέ[σσα]ρας χαλκοῦς ἐννέα (*BCH* lxvi–vii. 102 f.). A mass of material is contained in the fifth fascicule of *Fouilles de Delphes*, iii, in which are edited the Delphian financial records dating from the fourth century B.C. To collect and tabulate all the relevant references would serve no useful purpose, and I content myself with saying that in No. 15 we find examples, either actually preserved or capable of certain restoration, of χάλκεον, χαλκέους δύο, χ. τέτορας, χ. ὀκτώ, and χ. ἐννέα, while in Nos. 16 and 17, dating from 332–331 and 331–330 B.C. respectively, we find examples of 1, 2, 4, 7, 8, 9, and 10 χαλκοῦς, and elsewhere of 1, 3, 4, 5, 7, and 11 χαλκοῖ. Once, and once only, do we find χαλκοῖ ἕξ (28. 7), but this is fully accounted for by the numerous appearances of ἡμιωδέλιον or ἡμιωβέλιον. Only a single passage causes any difficulty, namely, 85. 19, where the editor, E. Bourguet, restores [ἐγρο]ά[ς ἐν τὸ] ἕλος χα[λ]κέοι (*sic*) δέκα ἐπ τὰ without offering any comment on the latter part of the phrase. Two courses are open to us, either (1) to write, as I prefer to do, χά[λ]κεοι δέκα. Επ - - (in this inscription there is no blank space or mark of punctuation between successive items), or (2) to admit that we have here a unique example of a number of χαλκοῖ exceeding twelve. Such an admission does not, however, necessarily invalidate the view that at Delphi 12 χαλκοῖ = 1 obol. We ourselves use the phrase "three halfpence" more frequently than "a penny halfpenny", nor should we be justified in inferring from the popular nursery-rhyme

> "You owe me five farthings"
> Say the bells of St. Martin's

that in the parish of St. Martin the number of farthings in the next higher denomination, the penny, exceeds five. For the Delphian money-system see further T. Homolle, *BCH* l. 26 f., 29 ff., T. Reinach, *BCH* li. 170 ff., H. Pomtow, *SIG* 239 note 8, 241 note 3, 250 note 19, 251 note 29 (178 note 8 requires correction), G. Glotz, *Rev. Ét. Gr.* xxxi. 88 ff.

For DELOS also the amount of evidence at our disposal is embarrassing and I cannot claim to have mastered it all. In the "Tabulae Archontum" (*IG* xi. 105–34) and in the "Tabulae Hieropoeorum" (*IG* xi. 135–289 and *Inscr. Délos*, 290–498) we have a large number of documents, many of them very voluminous, containing accounts and inventories of the Delian sanctuaries, in which values and weights are denoted by symbols of the acrophonic type, or, rarely, are written out in words (e.g., 154 *A* 49 ff. and *B*). In these the χαλκοῦς is indicated by / (earliest example, 145. 82 of 302 B.C.) or \ (earliest example, 226 *A* 9 of 257 B.C.) or — (e.g., 366 of 207 B.C.) or Ι (e.g., 401 *bis* of 190 B.C.), as well as by the strictly acrophonic Χ (earliest example, 146 *A* 64 of 301 B.C. or 165. 24 of about 280 B.C.). Occasionally two different signs occur in the same inscription, Χ and / in 146 (301 B.C.), 203 (269 B.C.), and 287 (250 B.C.), — and \, e.g., in 366 (207 B.C.), / and \, e.g., in 370 (203 B.C.). Ϲ is used throughout for the half-obol (except in 366, of 207 B.C., where it is replaced by <) and Τ for the quarter-obol. The sign of the χαλκοῦς is very frequently doubled, but I can find no example of its triplication, for the signs given as Ϝ/// in *BCH* xxviii. 160 *A* 16, of 173 B.C., appear in the revised edition (456 *A* 16) as ϹΧΧ. The conclusion is to my mind irresistible that the Delian obol contained 12 χαλκοῖ; if it were eight χαλκοῖ, the χαλκοῦς-sign would never require duplication, for ΧΧ would be replaced by Τ, while if it were sixteen, triplication would be fairly frequent in the representation of 3, 7, 11, and 15 χαλκοῖ.

I pass over without discussion the τρεῖς ὀβολοὺς τέτταρας | [χαλκοῦς] of *IG* xii (5) 1005. 5/6 (Ios, 3rd cent. B.C.) and the τε[τ]τάρων (?) ὀβολ[ῶ]ν [καὶ] δύο χα[λ|κ]ῶν of *IG* xii (7) 67. 5/6 (Arcesine on Amorgos, 4th or 3rd cent. B.C.), since these passages do not help us in our present inquiry, as well as the numismatic evidence above cited (Head, *Hist. Num.*[2] 601) for an obol of 8 χαλκοῖ at Chios, and I now turn to Asia Minor.

At CHALCEDON we find in *SIG* 1011. 5 a sum expressed by ϹΙΙ∶∶, where C represents the drachma, | the obol, and · presumably the χαλκοῦς. I have argued elsewhere (*JHS* xxxiii. 27 ff.; cf. *BSA* xviii. 120, xxviii. 147) that this evidence strongly suggests that at Chalcedon the χαλκοῦς was one-twelfth of the obol rather than one-eighth, as previously believed, and I still regard my reasoning as convincing.

PRIENE presents a problem which calls for examination. In a second-century document relative to the purchase of the priesthood of Dionysus we read ἐπρίατο Ἀθηνόπολις Κυδίμου δραχμῶν | μυρίων δισχιλίων δύο, καὶ τοῦ ἐπιδεκάτου δρα|χμῶν χιλίων διακοσίων ὀβολοῦ χαλκῶν | τριῶν (*Inscr. Prien.* 174. 35 ff. = *SIG* 1003. 35 ff.). The curious purchase price of 12,002 dr. is explained by Athenopolis' desire to secure the special privileges offered (ll. 27 ff.) to the purchaser if the sum paid should exceed 12,000 dr., i.e. 2 talents. On the basis of this passage Hiller von Gaertringen, with the approval of H. Winnefeld and B. Keil, concluded that at Priene 1 obol = 15 χαλκοῖ (*Inscr. Prien.* 174 note, *SIG* 1003 note 11), since the tithe (ἐπιδέκατον), payable immediately on the completion of the purchase (ll. 30 ff.), on 2 dr. is stated to be 1 ob. 3 ch. If, it is argued, $\frac{1}{10}$ of 2 dr. = 1 ob. 3 ch., then 2 dr. = 10 ob. 30 ch., and thus 30 ch. = 2 obols. This reasoning, though arithmetically unexceptionable, I unhesitatingly reject. It assumes (1) that at Priene we have a money-system of which no trace meets us anywhere else in the Greek world, and also (2) that the ἐπιδέκατον was calculated so as to be *precisely* one-tenth of the purchase-price. I cannot regard either of these assumptions as necessary or even probable. If at Priene 1 obol = 8 χαλκοῖ, the exact ἐπιδέκατον on 2 dr., i.e. 12 obols, would be 1 ob. $1\frac{3}{5}$ ch., and there would be no justification for charging 1 ob. 3 ch. rather than 1 ob. 2 ch.; but if, as I suppose to have been the case, 1 obol = 12 χαλκοῖ, the exact ἐπιδέκατον on two drachmas would be 1 ob. $2\frac{2}{5}$ ch., and, since there was probably at Priene no denomination lower than the χαλκοῦς, this might well be charged as 1 ob. 3 ch. Lack of precision in such reckonings is amply attested by the sums levied as purchase-tax (ἐπώνιον) in the Attic sale-lists (e.g. *IG* i². 325 ff.). Nor would the purchaser of the Prienian priesthood suffer any injustice; the ἐπιδέκατον was not an additional charge, like the Attic ἐπώνιον, but an initial payment, and the $\frac{3}{5}$ ch. which for the moment he lost he would recover later in the payment, in two instalments, of the balance.[12] I do not here attempt any explanation of the passage in another Prienian inscription (*Inscr. Prien.* 195. 20) where Hiller gives ΛΗΝ χαλκῶι ἑπτ' ὀβολούς. The reading is uncertain, and it is doubtful whether there is any reference to the χαλκοῦς.[13]

Of SYRIA, where some bronze coins of Antiochus IV Epiphanes (175–164 B.C.) bear on the reverse the value-marks $\overset{A\,B\,\Delta}{X\,X\,X}$, indicating 1, 2, and 4 χαλκοῖ respectively, and of EGYPT, where ostraka and papyri point to an obol of 8 χαλκοῖ (see above, p. 55, and Keil's note on *Inscr. Prien.* 174), I need not say more, for the epigraphical materials known to me add nothing to our knowledge.[14]

MARCUS N. TOD

---

[12] The interpretation given above has not been considered by Hiller in his note *ad loc.* The only alternatives which he suggests to what is in his judgement the "most probable" explanation, viz. that 1 dr. = 6 ob. of 15 ch. each, are (1) that 1 dr. = 8 ob. of 5 ch. each, or (2) that 1 dr. = 10 ob. of 3 ch. each. These suggestions appear to me to be not only less probable but wholly incredible. Moreover, the second is not even compatible with the passage which Hiller is discussing, for in that case the ἐπιδέκατον on 2 drachmas would be 2 obols and would certainly not be expressed as 1 ob. 3 ch. Since completing my final draft of the above paragraph on Priene, I have read K. Regling's discussion of the problem in *Die Münzen von Priene,* 122. He, too, rejects the theory of an obol containing 15 χαλκοῖ and summarily dismisses Hiller's two alternative suggestions, but, while inclining to the view that the Prienian obol = 12 χαλκοῖ, he holds that 16 χαλκοῖ is also possible, a view which I find it hard to share.

[13] Similarly, the χα[λκοῦς of *Inscr. Prien.* 163 probably has no reference to the coin so called.

[14] Pollux, ix. 80 f., refers to Aristotle's Ἀκραγαντίνων πολιτεία for the statement that at Acragas the λίτρα was the equivalent of the Aeginetan obol, and to his Ἱμεραίων πολιτεία for other names of Sicilian coins, οἷον οὐγκίαν, ὅπερ δύναται χαλκοῦν ἕνα, καὶ διξᾶντα, ὅπερ ἐστὶ δύο χαλκοῖ, καὶ τριξᾶντα, ὅπερ τρεῖς, καὶ ἡμίλιτρον, ὅπερ ἕξ, καὶ λίτραν, ἣν εἶναι ὀβολόν· τὸ μέντοι δεκάλιτρον δύνασθαι μὲν δέκα ὀβολούς, εἶναι δὲ στατῆρα Κορίνθιον. From the same source may well come Hesychius' gloss quoted above (footnote 9).

EPIGRAPHICAL NOTES ON
GREEK COINAGE

EPIGRAPHICAL NOTES ON GREEK COINAGE[1]

III. ΟΒΟΛΟΣ

FROM the κόλλυβος and the χαλκοῦς I pass to the ὀβολός and its multiples, together with those of its fractions which are expressed as subdivisions of the obol rather than as multiples of the χαλκοῦς. The primary meaning of ὀβελός is "spit", and in that sense the word occurs fourteen times in the *Iliad* and the *Odyssey* and once in the Homeric *Hymn to Hermes*, always in the dative or accusative plural. It is also found in this sense in two passages of Herodotus (ii. 41, 135), in several fifth-century poets (see LS), in an archaic Attic *lex sacra* (*IG* i². 842 *C* 4 ff. τρὲς ὀβελοί), and in a Coan sacrificial calendar of about 300 B.C. (*SIG* 1025. 53 αἱματίου ὀβελὸς τρικώλιος). In two places Herodotus uses ὀβελὸς λίθινος for "obelisk" (ii. 111, 170), while in Imperial times it usually denotes the critical sign, or "obelus". From this last meaning come the derivates ὀβελιαῖος, ὀβελίζω, and ὀβελισμός, while from the word in its primary sense come the diminutives ὀβελίσκος, denoting "skewer", "bar", "blade", "obelisk", "drainpipe", &c. (for references see LS)[2] and ὀβελισκολύχνιον. The meaning of ὀβελεία, found in several fourth- and third-century Attic records (*IG* ii². 1631. 409, 1672. 310, 1695. 14, 15), is uncertain, as is also that of ὀβελία (*SIG* 1000. 3 ; see Ziebarth *ad loc.*), and there is doubt, too, about the interpretation of ὀβελίας ἄρτος (sometimes ὀβελίας alone) and ὀβελίτης (see LS), sometimes taken as bread "baked or toasted on a spit", sometimes as a loaf "costing an obol". Athenaeus, iii. 111 B, says ὁ δὲ ὀβελίας ἄρτος κέκληται ἤτοι ὅτι ὀβολοῦ πιπράσκεται, ὡς ἐν τῇ Ἀλεξανδρείᾳ, ἢ ὅτι ἐν ὀβελίσκοις ὠπτᾶτο, and after quoting lines from Aristophanes and Pherecrates mentioning ὀβελίας (ἄρτος) he proceeds thus: ἐκαλοῦντο δὲ καὶ ὀβελιαφόροι οἱ ἐν ταῖς πομπαῖς παραφέροντες αὐτοὺς ἐπὶ τῶν ὤμων. Σωκράτης ἐν ϛ΄ Ἐπικλήσεων τὸν ὀβελίαν φησὶν ἄρτον Διόνυσον εὑρεῖν ἐν ταῖς στρατείαις. Pollux, vi. 75, derives the word

---

[1] For the previous notes of this series see *Num. Chron.* 1945, 108 ff., 1946, 47 ff. For the system of abbreviations here used see *Num. Chron.* 1946, 47, footnote 1.

[2] The meaning of the ὀ]βελίσκος (or -οι) found in a fifth-century inventory of the Eleusinian temple-furniture (*IG* i². 313. 141) is uncertain; LS translates "nail". Cf. *IG* ii². 1425. 407.

(rightly, in my judgement) from ὀβελός = "spit", when he speaks
of ὀβελίαι ἄρτοι οὖς εἰς Διονύσου ἔφερον οἱ καλούμενοι ὀβελιαφόροι, ἐκ
μεδίμνου ἑνὸς ἢ δυοῖν ἢ τριῶν τὸ μέγεθος, δι' ὀβελίσκων τινῶν εἰργμένους,
ἀφ' ὧν καὶ τοὔνομα.[3] I take it that these loaves, carried in proces-
sion in the cult of Dionysus, were of specially large size, somewhat
like the gigantic loaves which sometimes appear in our churches at
Harvest Festival services, and are not likely to have taken their
name from so modest a coin as the obol. In the entry in Bekker's
Anecdota Graeca, 111, ὀβολίας ἄρτους· τοὺς ὀβολοῦ πωλουμένους, the
spelling of the word seems to have been altered to support the
alleged meaning.

LS regards ὀβέλιος, cited from an inscription of Ilium, *CIG*
3597 *b*, as a variant form of ὀβελίας. The passage in question
appears in *CIG* thus:

- - - ἑκάστης] ἡμέρας ὀβολοὺς δύο καὶ πυρῶν χοίνικ α . . .

- - - ἄρτον] ὀβέλιον,

but we may note that the vital word ἄρτον is wholly restored, and
I am inclined to think that ὀβέλιον is either an otherwise unattested
diminutive of ὀβελός = "spit" or the latter part of a word denoting
a sum of money, perhaps ἡμι]οβέλιον.

Iron spits or skewers were an early form of currency in Sparta,
and elsewhere also spits of iron or other metal were similarly used.
Plutarch, *Lys.* 17. 5, says κινδυνεύει δὲ καὶ τὸ πάμπαν ἀρχαῖον οὕτως
ἔχειν, ὀβελίσκοις χρωμένων νομίσμασι σιδηροῖς, ἐνίων δὲ χαλκοῖς· ἀφ' ὧν
παραμένει πλῆθος ἔτι καὶ νῦν τῶν κερμάτων ὀβολοὺς καλεῖσθαι, δραχμὴν
δὲ τοὺς ἓξ ὀβολούς· τοσούτων γὰρ ἡ χεὶρ περιεδράττετο,[4] and the same

---

[3] Photius has two entries *s.v.* ὀβελίας ἄρτος, namely ὁ ἐπὶ ὀβελῶν ὀπτώμενος· λέγον-
ται δὲ καὶ ὀβελιαφόροι, οἱ ἐν τοῖς Διονυσίοις τοὺς ὀβελίας ἄρτους αἴροντες, and περιπεπλασμένος
μακρῷ ξύλῳ καὶ οὕτως ὀπτώμενος· γίνεται δὲ παραμήκης καὶ γαστρώδης. He does not
mention the alternative derivation. Cf. Eustath. pp. 951. 55, 1405. 26.

[4] Cf. *Etym. Magn. s.v.* ὀβελίσκος, ἐπειδὴ δὲ τότε (at the time of Phidon's recall
of the iron spits and issue of a silver currency) οἱ ὀβελίσκοι τὴν χεῖρα ἐπλήρουν,
τουτέστι τὴν δράκα, ἡμεῖς, καίπερ μὴ πληροῦντος τὴν δράκα τοῖς ἐξ ὀβολοῖς, δραχμὴν αὐτὴν
λέγομεν παρὰ τὸ δράξασθαι, Pollux, ix. 77 τὸ μέντοι τῶν ὀβολῶν ὄνομα οἱ μὲν ὅτι βουπόροις
ὀβελοῖς ἐχρῶντο πρὸς τὰς ἀμοιβάς, ὧν τὸ ὑπὸ τῇ δρακὶ πλῆθος ἐδόκει καλεῖσθαι δραχμή, τὰ
δ' ὀνόματα καὶ τοῦ νομίσματος μεταπεσόντος εἰς τὴν νῦν χρείαν ἐνέμεινεν ἐκ τῆς μνήμης τῆς
παλαιᾶς (cf. *Etym. Magn. s.vv.* δράγμα, δραχμή). Pollux then states Aristotle's
view, propounded in his Σικυωνίων πολιτεία, that the word was originally ὀφελός,
derived from ὀφέλλειν = αὔξειν, ἐπὶ μέντοι τῶν ὀβελῶν ὑπηλλάχθαι τὸ φ εἰς τὸ β κατὰ
συγγένειαν. See further W. Ridgeway, *The Origin of Metallic Currency and
Weight Standards*, 310, 346, and E. Boisacq, *Dictionnaire étymologique de la
langue grecque*², *s.v.* ὀβελός. The Aristotelian theory is accepted by the *Etym.*

writer, speaking of the poverty of Epaminondas, says οὐδὲν γὰρ οἴκοι τελευτήσαντος εὑρεθῆναι πλὴν ὀβελίσκον σιδηροῦν λέγουσι (*Fab. Max.* 27. 3). In the *Etymologicum Magnum, s.v.* ὀβελίσκος, we are told that πάντων πρῶτος Φείδων Ἀργεῖος νόμισμα ἔκοψεν ἐν Αἰγίνῃ· καὶ δοὺς τὸ νόμισμα καὶ ἀναλαβὼν τοὺς ὀβελίσκους, ἀνέθηκε τῇ ἐν Ἄργει ῞Ηρᾳ. I shall not here deal with the spits found in large numbers in the Argive Heraeum (C. Waldstein, *The Argive Heraeum*, i. 61 ff., ii. 300 ff.), nor with the seventh-century votive inscription from Perachora beginning Δραχμὰ ἐγό, ῞Ηρα λευϙ[όλενε, since they and the questions raised by them have recently been fully discussed by H. T. Wade-Gery (H. Payne, *Perachora*, i. 257 ff., No. 1, with photograph on Pl. 36 c and drawing on Pl. 132 iii); I simply call attention to the article (*CR* lviii. 18 f.) in which J. G. Milne argues that the object dedicated at Perachora consisted not of a bundle of six iron spits but of a silver Aeginetan drachma.

The word ὀβελός is used of a coin or a sum of money in the Athenian "Hekatompedon-inscription" of 485–484 B.C. (*IG* i². 3. 22 ὀβελ[ὸν ὀφ]λὲν, not cited in LS), but all later Attic inscriptions use in this sense the form ὀβολός, which first appears in the law, probably passed shortly before 460, regulating the Eleusinian Mysteries (*IG* i². 6). True, *IG* gives in l. 88 ὀ]βολ[όν (omitted from the index), in l. 95 ὀβελόν, and in l. 96 ὀ[βελόν, and LS therefore cites for ὀβελός = "obol" "*IG* I². 6. 95, al."; but the very careful revision of the text edited by B. D. Meritt (*Hesperia*, xiv. 61 ff.; cf. xv. 249 ff.) shows that the true readings are ὀβολ[όν] (l. 88 = *C* 5) and ὀβολόν (l. 95 = *C* 12), and he therefore restores ὀ[βολόν (l. 96 = *C* 13) and [ὀβο]λός (l. 97 = *C* 14). Apart from *IG* i². 3. 22, a Boeotian example noted below, and an entry in the second-century building-records of the temple of Apollo at Didyma (*Milet.* 7. 59, l. 6 f. γίνοντα[ι δραχμαὶ χ]ίλιαι ὀκτακόσιαι ἐξ ὀβελός),[5] I know of no epi-

---

Magn. s.v. ὀβελίσκος· οἱονεὶ ὀφελίσκος τις ὤν, ὁ εἰς μῆκος ὀφελλόμενος, τουτέστιν αὐξανόμενος· ὀφέλλειν γὰρ τὸ αὔξειν. Καὶ ὀβελός. Σημαίνει δὲ ἀμφότερα τὰς σούβλας. . . . ῞Οτι ὀβολὸς ἐκλήθη, ἐπειδὴ τὸ ἀρχαῖον τὸ χαλκοῦν νόμισμα τῶν Ἀθηναίων ὀβελίσκον εἶχεν. Φώτιος πατριάρχης . . . τροπῇ δὲ γίνεται τοῦ ε εἰς ο· πρὸ τούτου γὰρ ὀβελίσκοις τραχέσιν ἐνομίστευον. Οἱ μὲν οὖν ῞Ιωνες, ὀβελός· ἡμεῖς δέ, ὀβολός.

5 This may well be a mere error; in other accounts of the same temple construction we find ὀβολός (*Supp. Epigr.* iv. 450. 9, 453. 7). In a recently-published *lex sacra* from Paeania, dating from the second half of the fifth century B.C., ὀβολούς almost certainly means "spits" (W. Peek, *Ath. Mitt.* lxvi. 172). All editors wrongly restore [ὀβελόν] in a Coan law, *SIG* 1006. 12.

graphical example of ὀβελός = "obol", though a passage in a decree of Stymphalus is restored μὴ πλέον γε δυεῖν ὀ‖βελ]οῖν (*IG* v (2). 357. 158 f.), where I should prefer ὀ‖[βολ]οῖν or ὀ‖ δελ]οῖν. Of dialect forms of the word we find ὀδελός in Epicharmus (*fr.* 79 Kaibel, λέβητες χάλκιοι, κρατῆρες, ὀδελοί), in Aristophanes, *Acharnians*, 796, where it is put in the mouth of the Megarian, at Troezen in the compound ὀδελονόμος (*IG* iv. 757 *B* 42), at Epidaurus, if Hiller rightly reads and restores πέ]ντ' ὀδελῶν ἡμ[ιωδελίου (*IG* iv². 112. 18 f.), at Tegea (*IG* v (2). 3. 19, 24 ὀδελόν ... τρῖς ὀδελός), at Cretan Gortyn (*GDI* 4991 ii 13 ff. αἰ δέ κα δεδαμν[α]μέναν πε|δ' ἀμέραν, [ὀ δελόν, αἰ δέ κ' ἐν νυτ‖τί, δύ' ὀδελόνς, 4995. 7 [ὀδε]λὸν κατ' ἀμέραν, 5011. 4 f. τοδ‖ δ' ὀδελὸνς μὴ δέκετθαι τὸνς ἀργυρίος), Cnosus (*Inscr. Cret.* I. viii. 5 *B* 8 [τ]ριώδελον) and Eleutherna (*Inscr. Cret.* II. xii. 9. 3 τριόδελον), in Achaea ('Εφ. Ἀρχ. 1908, 95 μήτε χρυσίον ἔχεν πλέον ὀδελοῦ ὀλκάν), and at Delphi (*Delphes*, iii (5). 3 i 4, ii 36 τοῦ ὀδελοῦ τοῦ δευτ έρο]υ, in an account of 364–363 B.C., in which the word ὀβολός occurs twenty-one times; iii (5). 15 *passim*; *GDI* 2561 *D* 27, 29 ; *Schwyzer*, 322. 4, 5 δύ' ὀδελός, τέτορες ὀδελός; *BCH* lxvi–lxvii. 96 f.: cf. *Delphes*, iii (5). 4 iii 53, 15. 15 ἡμιωδέλιον).[6] In all the foregoing examples ὀδελός denotes a weight or a sum of money, save in the passages cited from Epicharmus and Aristophanes, where it means a spit ; Hesychius has the entry τριώδελον· τριῶν ἡμιμναίων σταθμός. In an early second-century inscription of Phalanna in Thessaly we find the phrase τοὶ] μεινὸς ἑκάστοι ὀβελλόν (*IG* ix (2). 1229. 20). Boisacq (*Dict. étym.* 682) gives ὀβελός as the Boeotian form of the word, but I can discover it only in one third-century inscription of Thespiae (*IG* vii. 1739. 8); in a dialect inscription of Orchomenus, dating from the late third and early second century B.C., ὀβολοί or ὀβολώς occurs eleven times (*IG* vii. 3193), in a list of dedications from the sanctuary of the Cabiri near Thebes we find ὁλκὰ δύ' ὀβολοί, ὁλκὰν ὀβολόν, ὁλκὰ δραχμὰ τρῖς ὀβολοί, ὁλκὰ τρῖς ὀβολοί, and a sum of money including πέντ' ὀβ⟨ολ⟩ώς (*IG* vii. 2420; cf. note 19 below), and in a long Orchomenian record of the late third century we have, if Lolling's reading, accepted by Dittenberger, is correct, δίου[ο] ὀβολίω (*IG* vii. 3172. 164), giving an otherwise unknown

---

[6] 'Οδελός = "obol" (weight) occurs also in Nicander, *Theriaca*, 655 τριπλόον ἐνθρύπτων ὀδελοῦ βάρος ἔνδοθεν οἴνης, which the scholiast explains τουτέστι τριώβολον, τρεῖς ὀβολούς.

form ὀβόλιον. For Hesychius' gloss ὀδολκαί· ὀβολοί. Κρῆτες, see P. Kretschmer, *Glotta*, ii. 326.

The obol is normally a silver coin, worth one-sixth of a drachma, but it may also consist of other metal. Thus in *IG* ii². 1672. 300 f., dated 329–328 B.C., ὀβολοὶ δύο χρυσοῖ are taken from the treasury of Demeter and from that of Core, while in *Inscr. Magn.* 121 a 10, 15, 19 we have [χ]άλκινον ὀβολό[ν], [χ]αλκίνους ὀβολ[ούς], and χάλκινον [ὀβ]ολόν. The legend ΟΒΟΛΟΣ occurs on bronze coins of Metapontum and Chios (Head, *H.N.*² 79, 601).

The change from ὀβελός to ὀβολός is due, Boisacq states (*loc. cit.*), to "une assimilation vocalique". This change of vowel also occurs in most of its derivatives. Of words clearly related to ὀβολός = weight or coin, we have ὀβόλιον (see above), ὀβολιαῖος, ὀβολισμός, ὀβολολογέω, ὀβολοστατέω, -ήρ, -ης, -ις, -ικός, the ὀβολίας of *AB* 111 (see above, p. 2), multiples of the obol, viz. τριημιωβόλιον, διώβολον, -ιαῖος, τριώβολον and derivates, τετρώβολον, -ος, -εῖος, -ιαῖος, -ίζω (the MS. of Photius has -βελίζων), πεντώβολος, -ον, -εῖος, ἑξώβολος, ἑπτώβολον, ὀκτώβολος, ἐννεόβολος (wrongly written for ἐννεώβολος), δεκώβολον, ὑπώβολος. On the other hand, words derived from ὀβελός = "spit" or "obelus" normally retain the -βελ-, as ὀβελεία, ὀβελιαῖος, ὀβελίας, -ίτης, -ιαφόρος (if rightly interpreted above, p. 1 f.), ὀβελίζω, -ισμός, ὀβελίσκος, -ισκολύχνιον (ὀβολίσκος is due to false analogy). But this principle is not consistently followed, for a number of words denoting coins or weights retain the original -βελ-, as ἡμιωβέλιον,[7] -ιαῖος, ἐμνιωβέλιον, διωβελία (once διοβελία), ἐπωβελία, ὀβελία, ὀβελλός, ὀδελός and all its compounds and derivates,[8] while we find -βολ- in at least two words derived from ὀβελός = "spit", the Homeric πεμπώβολον (see p. 17) and the Sophoclean ἀμφώβολος.

A further noteworthy characteristic of this group of words is the lengthening of the initial o to ω in compounds. This is a familiar phenomenon, designed to obviate too frequent a succession of short

---

[7] In *IG* iv²(1). 110 *A* 40 ἡ[μιωβ]ολίου appears, which Hiller von Gaertringen regards as a mere error, since elsewhere this and all other Epidaurian texts use only the form ἡμιωβέλιον. But ἡμιωβόλιον is found in Pollux, vi. 160, ix. 64, 65, 67, 87, and in Suidas *s.vv.* διώβολον (one MS. has ἡμιώβολον), ἡμιωβόλιον, Πάσης (the majority of the MSS. have -βέλιον). See LS *s.vv.* ἡμιωβελιαῖος, ἡμιωβέιουλ, ἡμιωβολιαῖος. In Hesychius the editors write ἡμιωβόλιον for the MS. ἡμιωβέλιον *s.vv.* ἥμαιθον, ἡμίεκτον, and for ἡμιβόλιον *s.v.* ἡμιωβόλιον.

[8] Ἡμιόδελος, marked as dubious in LS, is due to a misreading of the stone and must be disregarded.

vowels; thus we have φιλήνεμος from ἄνεμος, τριώνυμος from ὄνομα, τετρώροφος from ὄροφος, &c. This lengthening is almost invariably present in compounds of ὀβολός and ὀδελός alike, save in papyri and ostraca, where spelling is much less standardized. In literature and inscriptions, to which for the moment I confine myself, I know only the following exceptions: διοβελία in a letter of Hadrian (*IG* ii². 1103. 2), ἡμιοβόλιον in Paul. Aeg. 3. 29, ἡμιοβέλιν on coins of Aegium (Head, *H.N.*² 413),[9] τριόβολον (*IG* vii. 4139. 24 and Hesychius, *s.v.* ἄγκυρα) and τριοβολιμαῖος (Photius, *s.v.*). The words ἐννεόβολον and ἡμιόδελος (see note 8), included in LS, must be rejected, together with the [πεν]τοβόλους of *IG* xii (5). 878. 3 (see below, p. 17).

The single obol is almost always denoted by the singular noun ὀβολός in whatever case the context may determine; only rarely is εἷς added, as in *OGI* 674. 21 ὀβολὸν ἕνα (so in ll. 25, 31 δραχμὴν μίαν). Numerals either precede or follow the noun; thus in *OGI* 214. 36, 40, 45 we have τρεῖς ὀβολοί, but in l. 53 ὀβολοὶ τρεῖς without any difference of meaning or emphasis. and in *BCH* lxvi–lxvii. 96 τρὶς ὀδελούς and ὀδελοὺς τρὶς occur side by side.

I am impressed by the frequency with which the final short vowel of δύο, πέντε, ἑπτά, ἐννέα, δέκα, and ἕνδεκα is elided before the following ὀβολοί, even in inscriptions where elision is freely neglected. Thus, though δύο ὀβολῶν (*SIG* 1262. 4), πέντε ὀβολῶν (*IG* iv². 109 ii 160, 116. 15), δέκα ὀβολῶν (*ibid.* 109 ii 127) are not wholly unknown, they are very rare, and in *IG* v (1). 1433 the elision occurs in all fifteen possible cases. The treatment of the long final vowel of ὀκτώ is a different matter, and in the last-mentioned inscription, though once (l. 10) ὀκτ' ὀβολοί is written, in four cases (ll. 1, 2, 25, 27) the initial o of ὀβολοί disappears, leaving ὀκτὼ 'βολοί (see below, p. 19). It is almost certainly this form, coupled with the frequent combination ΔΥΟΒΟΛΟΙ (divisible as δύ' ὀβολοί or δύο βολοί)[10] which led to the occasional use of βολοί for ὀβολοί. Amphis, in his comedy *Πλάνος*, describes the rascally fishmonger as clipping his words (*fr.* 30 Kock),

οὐ λαλῶν ὅλα
τὰ ῥήματ', ἀλλὰ συλλαβὴν ἀφελών, "ττάρων
βολῶν γένοιτ' ἄν." "ἡ δὲ κέστρα;" "κτὼ βολῶν",

---

[9] The ἡμιοβέλιον of *IG* v(1). 1433. 1 is wrongly indexed (p. 344) as ἡμιοβέλιον.
[10] So, in our own language, "an adder" has arisen from "a nadder", "a newt" from "an ewt", "an apron" from "a napron", &c.

a passage which may have given rise to Hesychius' gloss βολοί· ὀβολοί.[11] This frequent elision is, I suggest, due not so much to a desire to secure euphony by the avoidance of hiatus as to the psychological feeling that numeral and noun cohere very closely and form almost a single word, δύ' ὀβολοί being the equivalent of διώβολον, and so on. Similarly we usually write "fourpence" or "sixpence" rather than "four pence" or "six pence", and our pronunciation of "twopence" or "threepence" differs markedly from that of "two pence" or "three pence".

Rarely do we find anything analogous to our abbreviated form of speech "two and sixpence", in which the next higher denomination, the shilling, is understood but not expressed; two Boeotian texts, however, which have been cited above, offer a number of examples (*IG* vii. 3172. 164, 3193 *saepe*), other instances occur in *IG* iv². 110 *A* 42, 45, 46, and one I think I have found in a fifth-century Athenian law (below, p. 10).

It is normally assumed that the obol referred to in any inscription is that of the state within which that inscription is engraved and exhibited. Sometimes, however, coins of foreign states appear in epigraphical records, especially as votive offerings, and their provenance is specifically indicated. Thus we have an ὀβολὸς Δελφι-κ[ός] in the Eleusinian treasury (*IG* ii². 1672. 300), while among the contents of the Delian temples are obols of Attica (*BCH* x. 464 l. 67; cf. *IG* ii². 1636. 24), Delos (*BCH* x. 464 l. 73), Orchomenus (*ibid.* 463 l. 59) and Phocaea (*IG* xi. 161 *B* 21), as well as the enigmatic ὀβολοὶ ἀρβυλικοί (*ibid.* 158 *A* 6, 159 *A* 72, 161 *B* 80, &c.; once, 199 *B* 19, written ἀγρολικοί), the nature of which is uncertain.[12]

---

[11] Or did Hesychius read τὼ βολώ rather than τὼ 'βολώ or τὼβολώ in Aristophanes, *Frogs*, 270? He seems (*s.v.* ὀβολοστάτης) to have read ὠ βολοστάται in Aristophanes, *Clouds*, 1155. Cf. the line of Crates quoted below in note 24.

[12] An ἀρβύλη was a walking-shoe or half-boot. LS translates ἀρβυλικός "in form of an ἀρβύλη", and T. Reinach says "fuerint oboli in hanc formam cusi, ut agrigentini nummi quidam dentium speciem, olbiani piscium referunt" (note on *IG* xi. 158 *A* 6). I suggest as a possible alternative that the coins in question bore an emblem which was understood, rightly or wrongly, as an ἀρβύλη. Hesychius' gloss μέλισσα· ὀβολός, ὅς ἐστι (ζ'), μέρος δραχμῆς refers, I suppose, to an obol bearing a bee as type (cf. Head, *Hist. Num.*² 571 ff., and Hesychius' gloss καλλιχέλωνος· ὁ ὀβολός).

Four special uses of the obol at Athens may be noted. (i) It was probably the earliest δικαστικὸς μισθός. Aristophanes, *Clouds*, 863, speaks of ὀβολὸν . . . ἡλιαστικόν, on which Photius comments ὀβολὸς ἡλιαστικός· ὃς τοῖς δικάζουσιν ἐδίδοτο, and Hesychius writes ὀβολοί· . . . καὶ ἐν ἄστει δικαστικοὶ μισθοί. (ii) It was the fee paid for attendance at the Assembly, the ἐκκλησιαστικὸς μισθός, as first introduced by Agyrrhius (Aristotle, Ἀθ. πολ. 41. 3). (iii) It was a recognized fee paid to soothsayers: cf. Photius, πελανοί· . . . καὶ ὁ τῷ μάντει διδόμενος μισθὸς ὀβολός. (iv) Aristophanes represents the fee due to Charon for ferrying the dead across the Styx as two obols (see p. 10 f.), but later authors repeatedly speak of one obol (Lucian, *De luctu*, 10 φέροντες ὀβολὸν ἐς τὸ στόμα κατέθηκαν αὐτῷ, μισθὸν τῷ πορθμεῖ. τῆς ναυτιλίας γενησόμενον, οὐ πρότερον ἐξετάσαντες . . . εἰ δύναται παρ' ἐκείνοις Ἀττικὸς ἢ Μακεδονικὸς ἢ Αἰγιναῖος ὀβολός, *Anth. Pal.* xi. 168. 6 ἐκ πολλῶν ὀβολὸν μοῦνον ἐνεγκάμενος, 171. 7 κεῖτο δὲ οὐδὲν ἔχων ὀβολοῦ πλέον, 209. 3 ἔχων ὀβολοῦ πλέον οὐδέν, Juvenal, iii. 267 nec habet quem porrigat ore trientem). Strabo says that Hermione regarded itself as lying especially near the nether world, διόπερ οὐκ ἐντιθέασιν ἐνταῦθα τοῖς νεκροῖς ναῦλον (viii. 6. 12; cf. Eustathius, 286. 44 f.). The most recent treatment of this phenomenon known to me is that by M. Guarducci, *Rendiconti della Pontificia Accademia*, xv. 87 ff.; cf. Waser, *RE* iii. 2177 f., LS *s.vv.* δανάκη, καρκάδων.

For the obol see also Babelon, *Traité*, i. 426 ff., Regling, *Wörterbuch der Münzkunde, s.v.* Obolos, W. Schwabacher, *RE* xvii. 1738 f.

I now pass to multiples of the obol, of which διώβολον, &c., are, strictly speaking, the neuter of the adjectives διώβολος, &c., with which the noun νόμισμα is understood.

ΤΡΙΗΜΙΩΒΟΛΙΟΝ. LS cites Aristophanes, *fr.* 48 (ἐν τῷ στόματι τριημιωβόλιον ἔχων), for this word, meaning "an obol and a half", i.e. a quarter-drachma. Pollux, ix. 64, quoting this line, says ἐν δὲ τῷ Ἀναγύρῳ τὰ τρία ἡμιωβόλια τριημιωβόλιον εἴρηκεν (*sc.* Ἀριστοφάνης). The word recurs in an abbreviated form on fifth-century silver coins of Corinth (*BMC: Corinth*, 10, Head, *H.N.*[2] 400 ΤΡΙΗ), Leucas (*BMC: Corinth*, 137 ΤΡΙ[Η]; cf. 142 ΤΡ) and Crane (Cranii) in Cephallenia (*BMC: Peloponnese*, 77, Head, *H.N.*[2] 427 ΤΡΙ). Normally it is replaced by τρία (or τρί') ἡμιωβόλια (Philemon *ap.* Poll. ix. 67 τρί' ἡμιωβόλι', Poll. ix. 87 δύνασθαι δὲ τὸν νοῦμμον τρία ἡμιωβόλια). To this form of expression Pollux elsewhere (ix. 55) draws attention, φίλον δὲ τοῖς ἀρχαίοις καὶ τὸ ἐν ἥμισυ τάλαντον τρία ἡμιτά-λαντα λέγειν, ὡς καὶ τρία ἡμίμναια τὴν μίαν ἡμίσειαν μνᾶν. So we also habitually use "three halfpence" in preference to "a penny half-penny". In inscriptions I have met only one example, the τρία ἡμιωβέλια (note the spelling with -βελ- instead of -βολ-) of Delphes, iii (5). 19. 17, a Delphian account of 361 B.C. For further numis-matic references see Babelon, Traité, i. 426, W. Schwabacher, RE vii A 142 f.

ΔΙΩΒΟΛΟΝ. LS registers διώβολον, "double obol", with its derivates διωβελία, "a daily allowance of two obols to needy citi-zens", διωβολιαῖος, "weighing two obols", and the irregular forms διοβελία and δυωβολιαῖος. For διώβολον it cites Aristophanes, Alexis, Theopompus Comicus, and Aristotle, Ἀθ. πολ. Διώδελον has not yet been found. The word διώβολον is surprisingly rare if we realize the frequency of δύ᾽ ὀβολώ, δύ᾽ ὀβολοί, and ὀβολοὶ δύο, a fact which seems to have struck Pollux, who, after mentioning the διώβολον, proceeds (ix. 63) ἀλλὰ τὸ μὲν τετρώβολον καὶ τριώβολον ἐν τῇ χρήσει τέτριπται· τὸ δὲ διώβολον ὡς ἐπὶ πολὺ λύοντες ἔλεγον, ὡς Δημοσθένης "ἀλλ᾽ ἐν τοῖν δυοῖν ὀβολοῖν ἐθεώρουν ἄν" κτλ. (Dem. xviii. 28). Pollux quotes (ix. 63, 64) the passages from Aristophanes' Αἰολοσίκων and Theopompus' Στρατιώτιδες which contain the word and remarks (ix. 62) ἦν τε καὶ τριώβολον καὶ διώβολον εἴδη νομισμάτων, but the preference for δύ᾽ ὀβολοί is exemplified in the Περὶ μέτρων καὶ σταθμῶν, 1 (Hultsch, Metrol. Scriptores, i, p. 207), where the series 1, 2, 3, 4 obols is expressed as ὀβολόν, δύο ὀβολούς, τριώβολον, τετρώβολον.

Διώβολον occurs in none of Aristophanes' extant plays, a curious fact in view of the frequent mentions in them of τριώβολον (see below), but Suidas refers to it s.v., Hesychius glosses ἥμαιθον· ἡμιω-βόλιον. διώβολον παρὰ Κυζικηνοῖς,[13] and in the Περὶ σημείων καὶ χαρακτήρων, 7 (Hultsch, Metrol. Scriptores, i, p. 226) the sign of the διώβολον is recorded. A difficult problem is presented by a phrase found in a mutilated Athenian law relative to the trierarchy, passed between 410 and 404 B.C. (Hesperia, iv. 15). The editor,

---

[13] For the ἥμαιθον (or ἥμαιθον), for which LS refers to the poets Herondas (iii. 45) and Phoenix of Colophon (ii. 3) and to Hesychius, see IG xii(1). 891 and note.

J. H. Oliver, reads in l. 10 - - - ος τὸ τριεράρχο ὀκτὸ διόβολο[ι] τὲς ἐμέρας h[εκ]άστε[ς - -, and comments (p. 19) thus: "In line 10 the reference to the daily eight diobols is not clear." I find it hard to accept ὀκτὼ διόβολο[ι] (or διώβολο[ι]), (i) because the use of the nominative case here, though possible, seems to me highly improbable; (ii) because the word διόβολος, or διώβολος, is unexampled, and (iii) because the phrase "eight diobols" is an unlikely way of expressing sixteen obols, i.e. two drachmas four obols. The first objection would be removed by restoring [ς] or [ν] in place of [ι] and regarding the word as an accusative or genitive plural, but the other two difficulties would remain. The care with which the text has been engraved and deciphered precludes the theory that the ancient engraver mistakenly wrote, or the modern editor wrongly read, διοβολο- for δύ' ὀβολο-. I see only one solution, to restore διόβολο[ν], i.e. διώβολο[ν], and to suppose that ὀκτώ gives the number of drachmas. Eight drachmas two obols is, we may note, exactly one-twelfth of a mina. If so, we have here an early example of a phenomenon mentioned above (p. 7). Curiously enough, the same problem arises in the study of a papyrus tax-receipt of 209 B.C. from Diospolis Magna, where Sammelb. 5729. 9 gives τέλος ὀκτὼ δυοβόλους δίχαλκον. Here, too, I believe, the word δραχμάς has been omitted and the text should read ὀκτὼ (sc. δραχμὰς) δύ' ὀβολούς.[14]

Among special uses of the diobol at Athens five call for notice. (i) It was the jurors' fee prior to the raising of the δικαστικὸς μισθός to three obols in 425 B.C.; (ii) it was the sum paid for attendance at the Assembly, as raised by Heraclides of Clazomenae (for whom see Kirchner, Prosopographia Attica, 6489) from the single obol instituted by Agyrrhius (ibid. 179), who later increased it again from two to three obols (Aristotle, 'Αθ. πολ. 41. 3); (iii) it was the daily sum paid from the θεωρικόν to a large number of citizens to pay for seats at certain of the great festivals, especially the dramatic competitions (see Busolt-Swoboda, Griech. Staatskunde, 1143 ff.); (iv) according to Aristophanes, it was the fee paid to Charon for his services as ferryman (Frogs, 140, 141 δύ' ὀβολώ, 270 ἔχε δὴ

---

[14] I now find that in this interpretation I have been anticipated by F. Ll. Griffith, Proc. Soc. Bibl. Arch. xxiii. 301. Δραχμάς is again omitted in the following line of the papyrus.

τὢβολώ, and probably *fr.* 3 διώβολον; cf. Apuleius, *Metam.* vi. 18 in ipso ore duas ferre stipes, and see above, p. 8); (v) in the impoverishment caused by the last phase of the Peloponnesian War, a daily dole of two obols was distributed to the poorer citizens.[15] This was called the διωβελία, and it appears twenty-one times[16] in the accounts of the period, *IG* i². 304, and has been restored with practical certainty for the suggested Δεκελείας in Xenophon, *Hell.* i. 7. 2 (the MSS. have διωκελίας or διωκελείας). Aristotle records its institution by the demagogue Cleophon, ὃς καὶ τὴν διωβελίαν ἐπόρισε πρῶτος· καὶ χρόνον μέν τινα διεδίδοτο, μετὰ δὲ ταῦτα κατέλυσε Καλλικράτης Παιανιεὺς πρῶτος ὑποσχόμενος ἐπιθήσειν πρὸς τοῖν δυοῖν ὀβολοῖν ἄλλον ὀβολόν (Ἀθ. πολ. 28. 3), but it is a mistake, I think, to refer solely to this subsistence-dole Aristotle's remark (*Pol.* ii. 1267ᵇ1 ff.) τὸ πρῶτον μὲν ἱκανὸν διωβολία (so all the MSS. read) μόνον, ὅταν δ' ἤδη τοῦτ' ᾖ πάτριον, ἀεὶ δέονται τοῦ πλείονος, for it may equally apply to the δικαστικός or the ἐκκλησιαστικὸς μισθός. Διωβελία has been doubtfully restored in *IG* ii². 657. 42 (= *SIG* 374. 42), and it recurs in the form διοβελία in a letter of Hadrian (*IG* ii². 1103), the mutilated condition of which prevents us from determining its exact meaning.

Of the adjective διώβολος I can find no example in Greek, unless in Alexis (*fr.* 186) we should read διώβολον (in place of διωβόλου) τοῦτ' ἐστί. In Latin, however, *diobolus* occurs once, side by side with repeated examples of *diobolaris*, meaning "cheap" (*Thesaurus Linguae Latinae*, v(1). 1223). Nor do I know any ancient evidence for the form διωβόλιον, though it occurs in the title of an article by F. Lenormant in Daremberg-Saglio, *Dictionnaire des antiquités*, ii. 224, and is used by Babelon, *Traité*, i. 425. The *Thesaurus* has the following entry: "Διωβόλιον, τό, demin. pro διώβολον, Duo oboli. Aristot. Polit. 2, 5 [this should read 2, 7]: Τὸ πρῶτον μὲν ἱκανὸν διωβόλια μόνον. [Διωβόλια Victorius posuit. Libri διωβολία. Vera scriptura est διωβελία, quod v.]" On διώβολον also the *Thesaurus* is

---

[15] Tod, *Selection of Greek Historical Inscriptions*, i, p. 206 f. Babelon (*Traité*, i. 425) wrongly identifies it with the ἐκκλησιαστικὸς μισθός when he says "La διωβελία, qui remplaça le τριώβολον ἐκκλησιαστικόν, était une gratification de deux oboles que l'État distribuait aux citoyens pour les indemniser d'avoir quitté leur travail lorsqu'ils prenaient part à l'assemblée du peuple."
[16] Only three references (ll. 10, 12, 45) are listed in the Index to *IG* i² (p. 349).

very weak, citing only two examples of the word, Aristophanes, *fr.* 3 and Alexis *ap.* Athenaeus, iii. 117 D.

With papyri and ostraca I am not qualified to deal, and I confine myself to a very few remarks. Preisigke's invaluable *Wörterbuch* gives (iii. 346 f.) a few references for διώβολον and a large number for δυόβολος, but A. S. Hunt in his copy queried the former entry, adding "these are only expansions", i.e. the word is not written in full but only indicated by the two-obol sign, while against the latter he added "?οι", rightly rejecting the form δυόβολος. In the indexes to Preisigke's *Sammelbuch* we find for vol. i the unhelpful "διώβολοι überall" (ii. 358), and for vols. iii and iv references to διώβολον in 6797. 2 ö., 7365. 1, 7450. 16 (iii. 346, iv. 150), but in all three passages the diobol is represented by a sign, not by a word. In other collections which I have examined, e.g. *Hibeh Papyri*, *Tebtunis Papyri*, *Oxyrhynchus Papyri*, the editors print the diobol-sign as (δυόβολοι) or (δυοβόλους).[17] This usage I find it hard to justify. The correct form of the diobol is διώβολον or δύ' ὀβολοί, but in papyri and ostraca -ωβ- might easily be turned into -οβ- and δι- into δυ-, giving rise to the form δυόβολον, doubly incorrect but perfectly natural and intelligible. It is this form which we find in Wilcken's *Griechische Ostraka*, ii. 371 ⊢ μίαν δυόβολ(ον), 1373 ⟨ πέντε δυόβ(ο)λ(ον), 1557 δυόβολ(ον), all three dated between A.D. 34 and 43, while once, in 385, we have ⊢ δέκα ὀκτὼι δυώβολ(ον).

For the diobol viewed from the numismatic standpoint see Babelon, *Traité*, i. 424 ff., Hultsch, *RE* v. 655 f., Regling, *Wörterbuch der Münzkunde*, *s.v.* Diobol.

ΤΡΙΩΒΟΛΟΝ. LS registers τριώβολον (with its Dorian equivalent τριώδελον) in two senses, (a) "three-obol piece, half-drachma", and (b) "a weight of three obols", to which we must add a third, namely (c) "the sum of three obols". It calls attention to four special uses of the τριώβολον at Athens, (i) as δικαστικὸς μισθός, (ii) as ἐκκλησιαστικὸς μισθός, (iii) as μισθός of the ἐπιβάται, or marines, and (iv) as a tax paid by metics. All the examples cited are taken from literature, most of them from comic poets (in Aristophanes alone the word occurs seventeen times), but for τριώδελον LS refers to an archaic inscription of Eleutherna in Crete, *GDI* 4957 *a* 3

---

[17] The (δυόβολους) of *PHib.* p. 286 is a mere misprint.

(now re-edited as *Inscr. Cret.* II. xii. 9. 3), al., and to Hesychius, who defines the word as τριῶν ἡμιμναίων σταθμός. Τριώβολον, though less frequent than τρεῖς ὀβολοί, is in common use to denote the half-drachma, for ἡμίδραχμον (for which see LS *s.v.* and add Pollux, ix. 62 τὸ δ᾽ ἡμίδραχμον καὶ τριώβολον ἂν καλοῖς, Hesychius τρίτον ἡμί-δραχμον· αἱ δύο δραχμαὶ καὶ τριώβολον, Photius τρίτον ἡμίδραχμον· τὰς δύο ἥμισυ δραχμὰς οὕτως εἰώθασιν ὀνομάζειν οἱ παλαιοί and τρίτον ἡμίδραχμον· δύο δραχμαὶ καὶ τῆς τρίτης ἥμισυ· ὡς εἶναι δύο δραχμὰς καὶ τριώβολον) seems never to have been popular. ΤΡΙꟼΒΟΛΟ|Ν| is found on a bronze coin of Samothrace (Head, *H.N.*[2] 263), ΤΡΙꟼ-ΒΟ[ΛΟΝ] on a leaden tessera (*BCH* viii. 10 No. 64 ; cf. Babelon, *Traité,* i. 372), and the word is found in various cases in inscriptions of Attica, *IG* ii[2]. 1414. 20, 1534. 233, 278, 1537. 17 (as a coin), 24 (as a weight), 1636. 30 (τ. Δήλιον) ; Epidaurus,[18] *IG* iv[2]. 109 ii 131, 137, 143, iii 33*, 80, 149, 110 *A* 26, 41, *B* 9*, 123. 107 ; Messene, *IG* v (1). 1433. 40*a* (see Add. p. 311) ; Thebes, *IG* vii. 2420. 39 (τ. Ἀττικόν) ;[19] Lebadea, vii. 3073. 12 ; the sanctuary of Apollo Ptoüs, vii. 4139. 24 (written τριόβολον) ; Delphi, *Delphes,* iii (5). 85. 17 ; Delos, *BCH.* x. 465 ll. 100 (Φωκικὸν τ.), 101 (Ἀττικὸν τ. *bis*),[20] 105 (Ἀττικὸν τ.) ; Rhodes, *IG* xii (1). 155. 23 ; and Arcesine in Amorgos, *IG* xii (7). 62. 23 = *SIG* 963. 23.

The coin in question is usually of silver, but I refer above to a bronze triobol of Samothrace, and in a long and detailed Eleusinian account of 329–328 B.C. we find τριώβολον χρυσοῦν . . . τριώβολον figuring in a list of coins removed from the treasury of Demeter (*IG* ii[2]. 1672. 300). The Dorian form τριώδελον occurs in a third-century Cnossian inscription (*GDI* 5072*b* 5, 8 = *Inscr. Cret.* I. viii. 5 *B* 5, 8) as well as in the aforementioned document of Eleutherna.

Of derivates of τριώβολον LS registers τριωβολιαῖος, "weighing three obols" or, in the colloquial sense, "twopenny-halfpenny" (see LS Add. p. 2108), τριωβολιμαῖος, "worth three obols", i.e. "worth-less" (Eustath. p. 1405. 28 τριώβολον, μισθὸς δικαστικὸς καὶ οἱ ἁπλῶς

---

[18] An asterisk indicates that the word is largely, or even wholly, restored.
[19] Recently re-edited in P. Wolters-G. Bruns, *Das Kabirenheiligtum bei Theben,* i, p. 22, No. 2.
[20] Wrongly indexed as τριωβέλιον Ἀττικόν, Φωκικόν, in W. H. D. Rouse, *Greek Votive Offerings,* 401.

τρεῖς ὀβολοί. ἐξ ὧν τριωβολιμαῖος, ὁ εὐτελής),²¹ and τριωβολεῖος "amounting to three obols (sc. per mina per month)", always applied to τόκος or τόκοι (nine examples are cited in Preisigke, *Wörterbuch*, iii. 354). It dismisses τριοβολιαῖος, of which it gives no example, and τριοβολιμαῖος, which is found in Photius, as *falsae lectiones* for τριωβ-, but admits τριόβολον, for which it cites *Sammelb.* 7378. 11, a papyrus of A.D. 103, and might have added the Boeotian inscription *IG* vii. 4139. 24 (see above) and Hesychius, ἄγκυρα· . . . Κύπριοι δὲ τὸ τριόβολον. In papyri and ostraca the triobol is usually represented by a symbol, but sometimes the word is written out in full (e.g. *Sammelb.* 6094. 13, a papyrus of 229–228 B.C., τριωβόλου) or in an abbreviated form (e.g. *Ostr. Strassb.* 73, of A.D. 51, τριό-β(ολον), 141, of A.D. 129, τριόβολ(ον)). Here the spelling τριοβ- is, so far as I can see, commoner than τριῶβ-.

Other occurrences, so far unmentioned, of τριώβολον in its mone-tary sense are found in Suidas, *s.vv.* διώβολον and τριώβολον (the former entry valueless, the latter long and, it seems to me, confused, failing to distinguish between the δικαστικός and the ἐκκλησιαστικὸς μισθός), Photius *s.v.* τρίτον ἡμίδραχμον, Pollux, ix. 62, 63, 66, 83, and *Sammelb.* 5729. 10 (a papyrus of 209 B.C.). As a weight it is men-tioned in the medical writers, Dioscorides, Antyllus, and Dieuches (Hultsch, *Metrologici Scriptores*, i, pp. 77 note 7, 82 note 3), in the Greek fragments of tables of weights and measures (*ibid.* pp. 207 l. 12, 226 l. 8, 244 l. 6), and in the scholiast on Nicander, *Theriaca*, 655 (see above, note 6).

For a numismatic account of the triobol see Babelon, *Traité*, i. 423 f., Regling, *Wörterbuch der Münzkunde*, *s.v.* Triobol, W. Schwa-bacher, *RE* vii A 160 f., whose reference to *IG* ii². 1672. 300 as "CIGAtt iv 834 b" betrays a singular lack of familiarity with even the most important of epigraphical collections.

ΤΕΤΡΩΒΟΛΟΝ. LS is, I think, unhappy in its treatment of τετρώβολος. Of the adjectival use, meaning "of four obols", it cites one example, the τετρώβολος τόκος of a Tenian inscription, *IG* xii (5). 860. 29, noting also the alternative form τετρωβολιαῖος, meaning

---

²¹ Suidas has τριωβολιμαῖος· τριῶν ὀβολῶν, εὔωνος. Photius and the *Etym. Magn.* give the same definition *s.v.* τριοβολιμαῖος. I am not convinced that Cobet is right in his contention (*Mnemosyne*, vii. 477) that we must either insert ἄξιος after ὀβολῶν or substitute ὤνιος for εὔωνος.

"priced at four obols", used by Suidas, *s.v.* τετρώβολον, and the scholiast on Aristophanes, *Peace*, 253. It then passes to the substantive τετρώβολον, to which it assigns two senses, (*a*) "four-obol piece", and (*b*) "weight of four obols", omitting the third and commonest meaning, (*c*) "the sum of four obols". For the first it cites Aristophanes, *Peace*, 254, accepting Kuster's emendation τετρωβόλου, rejected (rightly, in my view) by the Oxford editors, for the MS. reading τετρώβολον τοῦτ' ἐστί, in which τετρώβολον is an adjective, meaning "worth, or priced at, four obols". After citing two further examples of the substantival use (Polybius, xxxiv. 8. 8 τῶν δ' ἀρνῶν τριώβολον καὶ τετρώβολον ἡ τιμή, and a second-century Pergamene inscription, *SIG* 982. 15) LS proceeds: "it was a soldier's daily pay, hence τετρωβόλου βίος a *soldier's* life, Paus. Gr. *Fr.* 307; so in masc. τετρώβολος, of a common soldier, Men. *Pk.* 203" (κᾶν τετρωβόλους καλῆς), and records the use of τετρωβολίζω by Theopompus Comicus, 55 Kock, in the sense "receive four obols, i.e. to be a soldier". To me it seems probable that τετρωβόλου βίος means "the life, or livelihood, of a four-obol man, i.e. a soldier", rather than "the life of a four-obol piece", as interpreted by LS, and that here also the word is masculine rather than neuter. The reference to τετρωβολίζω also calls for a brief examination. Pollux, ix. 64, says παρὰ μέντοι Θεοπόμπῳ ἐν Στρατιώτισι καὶ τὸ τετρώβολον λαμβάνειν τετρωβολίζειν ὠνόμασται·

καίτοι τίς οὐκ ἂν εἰκὸς εὖ πράττοι τετρωβολίζων,
εἰ νῦν γε διώβολον φέρων ἀνὴρ τρέφει γυναῖκα;

Fritsch (followed by Kock, *Com. Att. Fragm.* i. 748) emends εἰκὸς to οἶκος. Photius explains τετρωβολίζων (the MS. reading is -βελ-) by τὸ δικαστικὸν τετρώβολον λαμβάνων· ἐγένετο γὰρ τοσοῦτον ποτέ, and Eustathius, p. 1405, 29, writes καὶ τετρωβολίζειν, τὸ λαμβάνειν δικαστικὸν τετρώβολον. ἐγένετο γάρ φασι καὶ τοσοῦτον ποτέ (cf. E. Schwabe, *Aelii Dionysii et Pausaniae Atticistarum fragmenta*, 211, No. 307). These two definitions are, however, unsatisfactory, for (*a*) τετρωβολίζων refers not to an actual but to a hypothetical payment, (*b*) the title of the play in which it occurs, Στρατιώτιδες, suggests a reference to the pay not of jurors but of soldiers, (*c*) Eustathius proceeds καὶ τετρωβόλου βίος παρὰ Παυσανίᾳ, ἀντὶ τοῦ στρατιώτου μισθός, and (*d*) we have no other evidence for any increase in the δικαστικὸς μισθός above the τριώβολον introduced in 425 B.C. in place

of the previous διώβολον. Kock suggests (loc. cit.) that the speaker
is pointing out that, if a woman were admitted to military service
as well as her husband and with equal pay, the family income (he
reads, as we have seen, οἶκος) would thereby be increased from two
to four obols daily. Otherwise we must suppose the sense to be
that a rise in the rate of pay (whether of juror or of soldier) from
two to four obols would make all the difference between straitened
means and comparative affluence.[22] In this connexion we may recall
two entries in Suidas, τετρώβολον· τουτέστι, πολυτίμητον· οὕτω δὲ
λέγουσι τὸ τετρωβολιαῖον, τουτέστι, τετρωβόλου πωλούμενον, and τεττάρων ὀβολῶν· ἐπὶ τῶν πολλῆς τιμῆς ἀξίων, and the scholium on
Aristophanes, Peace, 253, τετρώβολον· ἀντὶ τοῦ πολυτίμητον. οὕτω δὲ
κτλ. as in Suidas. I do not feel convinced, as do Kuster and other
scholars, that these three definitions say the exact opposite of what
is intended, and that in all of them οὐ must be inserted before
πολυτίμητον or πολλῆς. For the τετρώβολον as the soldier's pay see
also Eustathius, p. 951, 54, κεῖται παρὰ τοῖς παλαιοῖς καὶ τετρώβολον,
στρατιωτικός τις μισθός, Plutarch, Apophth. Lac. 233 c, Alcibiades,
35. 5, Lysander, 4. 5. Τετρώβολον meaning a sum of four obols
rather than specifically a four-obol piece is found also in inscriptions
of Epidaurus (IG iv². 108. 128 ; 109 ii 94, 99*, 107*; 110 C 1), of
Messene (IG v (1). 1433. 6, 40, 42) and of Coptus in Egypt (OGI
674. 32). In the asterisked passages the word is largely restored.
In a second-century text from Ilium (H. Schmidt, H. Schliemann's
Sammlung trojanischer Altertümer, 317, No. 9664 l. 9) [τε]τρώβολον
should be restored.

In papyri and ostraca τετρώβολον (or τέσσαρες ὀβολοί) is almost
always represented by a symbol; occasionally, however, it is
written out in full, as in Sammelb. 6997. 14 δρα]χμὰς τρεῖς ⸏τετρώβολον
ἡμιωβέλιον, or only slightly abbreviated, as in Ostr. Strassb. 145
τετρώβολ(ον). In the majority of examples it is written τετρόβολον,
as in BGU 953. 5 τετρόβολον (wrongly indexed as τετρόβολος in
Preisigke, Wörterbuch, iii. 354), Ostr. Strassb. 55, 60, 71, 75, 83, 197
τετρόβολ(ον) or τετρόβ(ολον) or τετρό(βολον). The word τετρωβολεῖος,
omitted from LS, occurs five times in two loan-contracts, one of
A.D. 184–9, now in Giessen (PGiss. i. 32. 5, 14 τόκων τετρωβολείων

---

[22] Babelon's translation, "Qui donc peut bien vivre en tétrobolisant ? "
(Traité, i. 423), seems to me very wide of the mark.

ἀργυρικῶν [ἑκάστης] μνᾶς κ[ατὰ μῆνα ἕ]καστον), the other of A.D. 151, now in Strassburg, which has, thrice over, an almost identical phrase, but with τόκου and τόκον in place of τόκων (PStrassb. i. 52. 3, 11, 13). For Attic silver tetrobols of the later part of the fourth century B.C. see Head, H.N.² 376, BMC: Attica, xxv, 16 and Pl. V. 12; for other coins of this denomination, Babelon, Traité, i. 422 f., Regling, Wörterbuch der Münzkunde, s.v. Tetrobol, RE v A 1099 f.

ΠΕΝΤΩΒΟΛΟΝ. LS cites the famous line of Aristophanes (Knights, 798) τοῦτον δεῖ ποτ' ἐν Ἀρκαδίᾳ πεντώβολον ἡλιάσασθαι, translating the adjective "at five obols a day"; Kuster proposed the emendation πεντωβόλου, the genitive of the substantive πεντώβολον.²³ LS also cites the phrase τόκος πεντώβολος from a Delian inscription, IG xi. 146 B 17 (in a papyrus of the second or third century A.D., Stud. Ital. xii. 106, we find the variant τόκου πεντωβωλείου, misspelt for πεντωβολείου), and κυλίκιον πεντωβόλου, "a cup of five-obol wine" from Lycophron, fr. 2. Among these examples of the adjectival use of πεντώβολος LS inserts the substantive πεντωβόλου, found in an Epidaurian building-record, IG iv². 109 ii 123. In a Tenian document, IG xii (5). 878. 3, we have πεν]τοβόλους, but the index (p. 364) registers this as "πεν]τοβόλους s. πέν]τ' ὀ." and I have no hesitation in reading πέν]τ' ὀβολούς here. In IG i¹. 324 a i 45, c ii 14, ΠΕΝΤΟΒΟΛΟΝ is transcribed πεντώβολον, but in the more recent edition of the inscription (IG i². 374. 98, 262) it is correctly transcribed πέντ' ὀβολόν. For Attic silver pentobols issued in the second half of the fourth century B.C. see Head, H.N.² 375, BMC: Attica, xxv, 15 and Pl. V. 11, J. N. Svoronos, Les Monnaies d'Athènes, Pl. 24. 1–9.

In Iliad, i. 463 (where see Leaf's note), and Odyssey, iii. 460, we find the phrase νέοι δὲ παρ' αὐτὸν ἔχον πεμπώβολα χερσίν, where πεμπώβολον means "five-pronged fork". The author of the "Herodotean" Vita Homeri, 37, has this comment: Αἰολέες γὰρ μόνοι τὰ σπλάγχνα ἐπὶ πέντε ὀβελῶν ὀπτῶσιν, οἱ δὲ ἄλλοι Ἕλληνες ἐπὶ τριῶν. καὶ γὰρ ὀνομάζουσιν οἱ Αἰολεῖς τὰ πέντε πέμπε. From Suidas' gloss quoted in note 23 it would appear that sometimes this word was used to denote a five-obol piece.

---

²³ The MS. reading is confirmed by Suidas' gloss πεντώβολον ἡλιάσασθαι· νικήσαντα τοὺς Πελοποννησίους, δικάσαι μέχρις Ἀρκαδίας, λαμβάνοντα μισθὸν πεντώβολον, ἀλλ' οὐ τριώβολον. Καὶ πεμπώβολον ὁμοίως.

ΕΞΩΒΟΛΟΝ. The noun does not, so far as I know, occur in inscriptions, for the simple reason that for six obols the Greek would normally write one drachma. The adjective ἑξώβολος, however, is found, meaning "consisting of six obols", in Hesychius, λεπτὰς καὶ παχείας· Ζάλευκος ἐν Νόμοις τὰς δραχμάς· λεπτὰς μὲν τὰς ἑξωβόλους, παχείας δὲ τὰς πλέον ἐχούσας (cf. παχείᾳ δραχμῇ· τὸ δίδραχμον. Ἀχαῖος). The word is omitted from the *Thesaurus* and from LS, and is wrongly written ἑξωβόλους in the standard edition of Hesychius, that of M. Schmidt. Not that the phrase ἓξ ὀβολοί is wholly inadmissible, especially in places where the stater and not the drachma is the unit of reckoning. In *Delphes*, iii (5). 48 ii 42, it is restored with practical certainty, and in an inscription of Magnesia on the Maeander ὀ]βολοὺς ἓξ occurs (*Inscr. Magn.* 121 *b* 2). Nevertheless, its rarity at Delphi is in striking contrast to the frequency of ὀβολοὺς ἑπτά, ὀκτώ, ἐννέα, δέκα, and ἔνδεκα, and I find no example of it in the extensive Epidaurian accounts, though there are occasional appearances of δέκα (*IG* iv². 109 ii 127, 110 *A* 38) and ἔνδεκ᾽ ὀβολῶν (iv². 109 i 129, 110 *A* 17). It is noteworthy, too, that in the Messenian financial record *IG* v (1). 1433 we find sums of money containing 1, 2, 3, 4, 5, 7, 8, 9, 10, and 11 obols, but in the one case (l. 9) where 6 obols might have been expected we have δραχμά, the only appearance of that word in this long inscription. So we very rarely speak of "twelve pence", whereas "fifteen pence" and "eighteen pence" are in frequent use. In an ostracon from Egyptian Thebes, dated A.D. 40, ἐ]ξόβολ(ον) and ἑξόβ(ολον) occur (*Ostr. Strassb.* 67), but this incorrect spelling with -οβολ- in place of -ωβολ- is very common in ostraca and papyri in all the multiples of the obol. For this Egyptian coin see Babelon, *Traité*, i. 422; there is no entry *s.v.* Hexobol in *Wörterbuch der Münzkunde* or in *RE*.

ΕΠΤΩΒΟΛΟΝ. I know of no epigraphical evidence for this Ptolemaic coin, for which see Babelon, *Traité*, i. 421, Regling, *Wörterbuch der Münzkunde, s.v.* Heptobol.

ΟΚΤΩΒΟΛΟΝ. LS has the following entry: "ὀκτώβολοι, οἱ, *eight obols, IG* 5 (1). 1433 (Messene); also ἁ ὀκτώβολος εἰσφορά *tax of eight obols per mina,* ib. 1432. 3 (i A.D.)." The phrase ὀκτώβολος εἰσφορά recurs *ibid.* 1433. 28, 30; its meaning is discussed by A. Wilhelm, *Jahresh.* xvii. 48 ff. The two inscriptions were assigned by their editor, W. Kolbe, on the ground of their script, to the first century B.C. or rather A.D. (see *lemma* of 1432), and he identified "Memmius the proconsul" (1432. 36) with P. Memmius Regulus, who was consul in A.D. 31 and subsequently governed Achaea, Macedonia, and Moesia. Wilamowitz, however, attributed them to the time when Antonius was levying money for his Asiatic war, and added "litteras quoque his temporibus recentiores esse minime credo" (commentary on 1432), and in Plate IV Kolbe dated both inscriptions in 39 B.C. I cannot accept the word ὀκτώβολοι given by Kolbe in 1433. 1, 2, 25, 27 and registered in LS; in all these places I should write ὀκτὼ 'βολοί (see above, p. 6), while in l. 10 Kolbe himself rightly gives ὀκτ' ὀβολοί.[24] For the issue of eight-obol pieces, almost confined to the cities of Euboea, see Regling, *Wörterbuch der Münzkunde*, *s.v.* Oktobol, and W. Schwabacher, *RE* xvii. 2393.

ΕΝΝΕΩΒΟΛΟΝ. LS cites ἐννεόβολον (*sic*), "sum of nine obols", from an Oropian *lex sacra* of the fourth century B.C. (*IG* vii. 235. 22 = *SIG* 1004. 22), which is also cited by Babelon, *Traité*, i. 421. But a careful revision of the stone by B. Leonardos showed that the true reading is ἐννέ' ὀβολούς (*Ἀρχ. Ἐφ.* 1917, 232 ff.; cf. *Schwyzer*, 811. 22 and note). In *BGU* 1161. 10 f., a Berlin papyrus of 24–23 B.C., Schubart gives τόκων ἐννεοβολῶν [τῆς μνᾶς ἑκάσ]|της τοῦ μηνὸς ἑκά[στου], and this is indexed under ἐννεοβολός (*BGU* iv, index, p. 19; so also Preisigke, *Wörterbuch*, iii. 347). I prefer to write ἐννεοβόλων (incorrectly spelt for ἐννεωβόλων) and to derive it from the adjective ἐννεώβολος, not recognized by LS. Preisigke (*loc. cit.*) also cites *BGU* 1147. 8, an Alexandrian loan-contract of 13 B.C., also edited in Wilcken, *Chr.* ii (2). 125, No. 103, for the phrase δάνειον τόκων ἐννεωβολῶν (*sic*), and though the said papyrus had, as originally published, δάνειον . . . τόκων τριωβόλων, a later revision by Schubart established ἐνεωβόλων, a misspelling of ἐννεωβόλων, as the true reading (Preisigke, *Berichtigungsliste*, 98), and this is incorporated in the text edited by P. M. Meyer (*Juristische Papyri*,

---

[24] We may further note Harpocr. ἐπιτρίταις· . . . ἀντὶ τοῦ ἐπὶ η' ὀβολοῖς, κατὰ τὸ τρίτον εἶναι μέρος τοὺς η' ὀβολοὺς τοῦ τετραδράχμου, Hsch. σίγλον· νόμισμα Περσικὸν δυνάμενον ὀκτὼ ὀβολοὺς Ἀττικούς, Phot. σίκλος· . . . σταθμὸς βαρβαρικὸς δυνάμενος ὀκτὼ ὀβολοὺς Ἀττικούς, Poll. ix. 62 οἱ ὀκτὼ ὀβολοὶ ἡμίεκτον ὠνομάζοντο, in support of which statement Pollux quotes a line of Crates' Lamia (*fr.* 20 Kock) ἡμίεκτόν ἐστι χρυσοῦ, μανθάνεις, ὀκτὼ 'βολοί.

149, No. 45). Even in Attica ἐννέ' ὀβολοί can be used to denote 1½ drachmas (Aristophanes, *Frogs*, 177), and elsewhere this phrase is not uncommon.

ΔΕΚΩΒΟΛΟΝ. LS cites only *IG* ii. 837. 23, now re-edited as *IG* ii². 1537. 23, where a δεκώβο[λον], a 10-obol piece, figures in a list of gifts offered in the Athenian Asclepieum. I do not understand Regling's remark "nur als Rechnungsgrösse, nicht als geprägtes Stück" (*Wörterbuch der Münzkunde, s.v.* Dekobolon; cf. Babelon, *Traité*, i. 421), for the word seems to me to denote a single object, and not simply, as in a third-century Epidaurian building-record (*IG* iv². 109 ii 114), the sum 1 dr. 4 ob. Possibly the rarity of the coin enhanced its interest and so made it worthy to rank among the possessions of the god side by side with the more costly offerings recorded in the same inscription. Aristophanes, *Wasps*, 1391, uses δέκ' ὀβολῶν as a more convenient phrase than δραχμῆς τεττάρων ὀβολῶν.[25]

Higher multiples of the obol are not known to me, though we find ἔνδεκ' [ὀ]βο[λῶν] and ἔνδε[κ' ὀβο]λῶν at Epidaurus (*IG* iv². 109 i 129, 110 *A* 17). In a third-century treaty between Aetolia and Acarnania we have, according to *SIG* 421. 39 f., τῶι [δὲ] τὰμ πανοπλίαν ἔχο||[ντι δώδεκ' ὀβολοί], τῶι δὲ τὸ ἡμιθωράκιον ἐννέ' ὀβολοί, ψιλῶι ἐπτ' ὀβολοί, but Klaffenbach (rightly, I think) restores δύο δραχμαί in place of δώδεκ' ὀβολοί (*IG* ix²(1). 3. 40). Photius has a doubtful gloss σίκλος· ὀβολοὶ εἴκοσι, and an Oropian inventory of about 240 B.C. registers an offering of ὀβολοὶ ΔΔ (*IG* vii. 303. 101).

I now turn to fractions of the obol which are not expressed as multiples of the χαλκοῦς.

HMI(TE)TAPTHMOPION (⅛-obol) does not, so far as I know, occur in literature or inscriptions, though found in the abbreviated form HE on bronze coins of Metapontum (Head, *H.N.*² 80); in states such as Attica, where the obol consisted of eight χαλκοῖ, the word χαλκοῦς was used as being shorter and simpler, though the surviving Attic ἡμιτεταρτημόρια are silver coins. See Babelon, *Traité*, i. 435 f.; there is no entry *s.v.* in *RE*.

TETAPTHMOPION, from which are derived the adjectives τεταρτημόριος and -μοριαῖος (see LS), meant "a quarter" (as did

---

[25] Cf. Poll. ix. 81 τὸ μέντοι δεκάλιτρον δύνασθαι μὲν δέκα ὀβολούς, εἶναι δὲ στατῆρα Κορίνθιον. In *IG* iv²(1). 109 ii 127, 110 *A* 38 we have δέκα (or δέκ') ὀβολῶν.

also τεταρτημορίς, *SIG* 1015. 11, 1044. 39), but was used in especial for ¼-obol as a weight, coin, or value, or for ¼-cotyle as a measure (see also Hultsch, *Metrol. Script.* ii. 220). In the wider sense it occurs, e.g., in Hdt. ii. 180 and in Pollux, ix. 56, who speaks of τριτημόριον ταλάντου καὶ τεταρτημόριον; in the narrower it is found in Aristotle and Plutarch (see LS) as well as in the lexicographers Harpocration, *s.v.* (τὸ τέταρτον μέρος τοῦ ὀβολοῦ, τουτέστι χαλκοῖ β'), Pollux, ix. 65 (οἱ μὲν δύο χαλκοῖ τεταρτημόριον . . . ὠνομάζετο), Hesychius, *s.v.* (οἱ δύο χαλκοῖ), Photius, *s.v.*, the *Etymologicum Magnum*, *s.v.*, and Suidas, *s.v.* (δίχαλκον. ὁ γὰρ χαλκοῦς ὄγδοον τοῦ ὀβολοῦ. καὶ τεταρτημόριόν τινα καλοῦσιν, οἷον διχάλκου ἄξιον. This meaning of the adjective should be added to LS) and *s.v.* τριτημόριον. In the early fourth century B.C. τετα[ρτη]μόριον is found in the Delphian law of Cadys.[26]

The word occurs equally often in the syncopated form ταρτημόριον. Pollux, ix. 65, speaks of τεταρτημόριον καὶ κατὰ ἀποκοπὴν ταρτημόριον. Harpocration and Suidas do not mention it, but it occurs in Hesychius, Photius, and the *Etymologicum Magnum*, *s.v.*, and we find the epithets ταρτημόριος and ταρτημοριαῖος in the sense of διχάλκου ἄξιος, "of little worth", the former in the *Etymologicum*, the latter in Photius. To the references for ταρτημόριον given in LS we may add *Inscr. Délos*, 1442 A 32 (where ταρτήμόρι[ον] is a coin), 44 (ἐνώι[δια ὣ]ν ὁλκὴ ὀβολοὶ δύο ταρτημόριον, where it is a weight), and for ταρτήμορον *Inscr. Délos*, 320 B 66 (κασσιτέρου ῥάβδοι τρεῖς ταρτήμορον, ὁλκὴ μναῖ ΔΔΓΙΙ, where it means "a quarter") and *IG* ii². 1013. 54 f. (revised by B. D. Meritt, *Hesperia*, vii. 129), where it is ordered that σηκώματα τοῦ τ[ε] ἐμπορι[κ]οῦ [ταλάν|το]υ καὶ δεκάμνου ⟨καὶ πεντάμνου⟩ καὶ δίμνου [καὶ μνᾶς] καὶ ἡμιμναίου καὶ τα[ρ]τημόρου καὶ χοός [καὶ χοίνικος] shall be deposited on the Acropolis. Here the word clearly means ¼-mina.[27] For numismatic accounts of the quarter-obol see Babelon, *Traité*, i. 434 f., K. Regling, *RE* V A 1064 f.

---

[26] So read and restored by E. Bourguet, *Delphes*, iii (1). 294. 19, following T. Homolle, *BCH* l. 15, and T. Reinach, *BCH* li. 173, but in the light of *Delphes*, iii (5). 78. 7, I should prefer to write τετα[ρτα]μόριον.

[27] In *Delphes*, iii (5), p. 275, E. Bourguet says that "la forme ταρτημόριον se trouve à Athènes (*IG*, II, 741 c [this should read *Bc*], 13; cf. *Bull. Soc. Ling.*, 29, 111)". The reference is to *IG* ii². 1496. 207, where, as indicated in LS, it is uncertain whether ταρτημό[ριον] or ταρτήμο[ρον] should be restored.

TPIHMI(TE)TAPTHMOPION, which forms the title of articles by Babelon (*Traité*, i. 433 f.) and W. Schwabacher (*RE* vii A 143 f.), is, so far as I know, a modern word without ancient authority. Though a silver coin, it was probably called τρίχαλκον at Athens. *HMIΩBEΛION* is the usual spelling of the ½-obol, attested not only by several authors (see LS). but by inscriptions of Attica (*IG* i². 6. 90 = Meritt, *Hesperia*, xiv. 77 *C* 7 [before 460 B.C.], 140. 2 [5th cent., restored], ii². 1414. 6, 7 [early 4th cent.], &c.), Epidaurus (*IG* iv². 106 iii 83 ; 109 ii 126, 143, 157, 160 ; 110 *A* 26. 35, &c. ; the index is very incomplete), Messene (*IG* v (1). 1433. 1 [1st cent. B.C.], wrongly indexed as ἡμιοβ-), Thebes (*IG* vii. 2406. 16), Delphi (*Delphes*, iii (5). 3 i 52, 54, ii 13, 52 ; 16. 15, 18, 50 ; 19. 18, 27, 46, 50, 70, &c. [all 4th cent.]), Delos (*BCH* x. 463, 465 [364 B.C.], *IG* xi. 138 *B* 10 [late 4th cent.], 203 *A* 30, &c.), Cos (*SIG* 1006. 11 [3rd cent.]), Ceos (*IG* xii (5). 530. 8, where KIΠBEΛIONOΣ almost certainly conceals ἡ]⟨μ⟩ιωβέλιον),Pergamum (*SIG* 982. 25 [2nd cent.]) and Priene (*Inscr. Prien.* 140. 5, 12 [early 3rd cent.]). The dialect form ἡμιωδέλιον occurs at Delphi (*Delphes*, iii (5). 4 iii 53 [361 B.C.], 15. 15 [4th cent.]) and Taras (*IG* xiv. 2406. 77, 87) and is restored with tolerable certainty in an Epidaurian account of the fourth or third century (*IG* iv². 112. 18 f.), while ἐμνιωβέλιον appears in a third-century document of Acraephia in Boeotia (*Supp. Epigr.* iii. 356. 5, 7). The derivate adjective [ἡμιω]βελια[ῖος] is found in a third-century papyrus (*PCair. Zen.* 59019. 5), and ἡμιοβέλιον occurs on an ostracon of A.D. 15 (*Ostr. Strassb.* 55) and HMIOBEΛIN on a bronze coin of Aegium (Head, *H.N.*² 413 ; cf. Grose, *McClean Collection*, 6318). 'Ημιόδελος, registered in LS as "dub. in *GDI* 2562. 26 (Delph., iv B.C.)", is due to a faulty copy made by Dodwell and must be deleted (*Delphes*, iii (5). 15. 15). For the corresponding forms with -βολ- in place of -βελ- see above (p. 5 and note 7). The diminutive ending -ιον is probably due to the pettiness of the value or weight indicated and extends to τριημιωβόλιον, but it is not found in the higher values, διώβολον, τριώβολον, &c., and to their analogy we may attribute the form ἡμιώβολον which is occasionally used (see LS).²⁸

---

²⁸ For the word διωβόλιον see above, p. 11 ; τριωβέλιον is an invention of Rouse (*Greek Votive Offerings*, 401). 'Ημιώβολον is written in full in several passages of the "Fragmenta de mensuris cavis ac ponderibus" (Hultsch,

With papyri and ostraca, the fluidity and capriciousness of whose spelling seems to have infected in some measure even the scholars who study them, I do not here deal at all fully. Thus in the index of Wilcken's *Griechische Ostraka* (ii, p. 489) I find under ἡμιόβολον eleven references to ostraca of the first two centuries A.D., but investigation shows that in none of them is the word written out in this form : we have ἡμιοβόλιον, ἡμιοβέλιν, ἡμιώβολον written in full and the abbreviations ἡμιοβ., ἡμιωβ., ἡμιο. (twice), ἡμιλ., and ἡμ., while in the tenth case Wilcken writes ἡ[μιώ(βολον)] (corrected in A. S. Hunt's handwriting to ἰμιώ[βολον]) and in the eleventh the whole word is restored [ἡμιώβολον] : thus in only one of the eleven examples are we bound to accept the ending -λον instead of -λιον, -λιν. In P. M. Meyer's edition of the Hamburg papyri the index (i, p. 259) gives ἡμιωβέλιον, but in all the cases cited the word is indicated by the symbol S and appears as (ἡμιόβολον) in 3 *A* 8, 9, *B* 6, but as (ἡμιωβέλιον) in 114 *passim*. Preisigke's *Wörterbuch*, again, gives (iii. 348) a considerable number of examples of ἡμιώβολον, but in every one of them a symbol is used and so there is in them no evidence for ἡμιώβολον rather than for ἡμιωβέλιον (rarely misspelt ἡμιοβέλιον or -βόλιον). Occasionally ἥμισυ is used in place of ἡμιωβέλιον, as in a Leningrad ostracon of the second century A.D. (*Arch. Pap.* v. 173, No. 10. 6 ὀβολοὶ δύο ἥμισυ δίχαλκον) and in another ostracon dated A.D. 175 (*Sammelb.* 7394. 6 ὀβολ(οὺς) δύο ἥμισυ) ; cf. Hesychius ἥμισυ· . . . ἔστι δὲ καὶ νόμισμά τι.

The half-obol was a silver coin, though we have seen that at Aegium there were bronze coins stamped ἡμιοβέλιν. In *IG* ii². 1388. 70 we find among the treasures of Athena in 398–397 B.C. χρυσὸν : Ϲ:, i.e. χρυσοῦν ἡμιωβέλιον, and in a later list we have χρυσοῦν ἡμιωβέλιον and ἡμιωβέλιον χρυσοῦν (*IG* ii². 1414. 6, 7). In an inventory of the Delian temple-treasures we have a record of Ἀττικὰ δύο ἡμιωβέλια (*BCH* x. 465 l. 106 ; cf. *IG* ii². 1642. 24 ἡμιωβέλια π[έν]τε).

For the half-obol see further Babelon, *Traité*, i. 432 f., Viedebantt, *RE* viii. 249 ff., where (250 init.) *IG* vii. 2406 should be read for *IG* vii. 406 and the reference to ἡμιώδελος should be deleted.

TPITHMOPION. LS registers the adjectives τριτημόριος and

Metrol. Script. ii. 180 *s.v.*, where 237 should be read for 337), where the form ἡμβόλιον also occurs (*op. cit.* ii. 178 *s.v.*, where 319, 4 should be read for 319, 1).

-μοριαῖος, meaning "equal to a third part", and the substantive τριτημόριον, used by Herodotus (ix. 34), Thucydides, and other writers to denote "third part" (we have seen that Pollux, ix. 56, speaks of τριτημόριον ταλάντου): normally Herodotus uses τριτημορίς in this sense, and this form of the word recurs in Dio Cassius. Τριτημόριον appears in the lexicographers with the meaning "three-quarters of an obol". Thus Harpocration has τριτημόριον· Δείναρχος κατὰ Καλλισθένους. ὅτι δὲ τριτημόριόν ἐστιν ϛ′ χαλκοῖ Φιλήμων ἐν ἀρχῇ τοῦ Σαρδίου διδάσκει, and Photius has the same entry save that he omits ἐν ἀρχῇ τοῦ Σαρδίου, while elsewhere he writes τοὺς ἐξ χαλκοῦς εἴρηκεν Φιλήμων τοῦ ὀβολοῦ τριτημόριον, a phrase repeated verbally in Suidas, and the Etymologicum Magnum has (s.v. τεταρτημόριον) τριτημόριον δὲ τοὺς ἐξ χαλκοῦς εἴρηκε Φιλήμων. In Pollux (ix. 65 f.) we read οἱ δ᾽ ἐξ (sc. χαλκοῖ) τριτημόριον, ὅτι τὰ τρία μέρη ἐστὶ τοῦ ὀβολοῦ . . . ὅτι δὲ τοὺς ἐξ χαλκοῦς τριτημόριον ὠνόμαζον, ἔστιν εὑρεῖν ἐν τῷ Φιλήμονος Σαρδίῳ, which he proceeds to quote, as also a passage in the same poet's Πιττοκοπούμενος, and Hesychius defines τριτημόριον as οἱ ἐξ χαλκοῖ and elsewhere speaks of the word as applied ἐπὶ νομίσματος ἀργυρίου (should this not be ἀργυροῦ?). In two places, however, Hesychius seems to be at fault, for he writes ταρτημόριον· τὸ τριτημόριον, ἢ τὸ δίχαλκον ·and δανάκης· νομισμάτιόν τι βαρβαρικόν, δυνάμενον πλέον ὀβολοῦ ὀλίγῳ, τριτημόριον.

There can be no doubt that τριτημόριον = ¾-obol or (in states where the obol comprised eight χαλκοῖ) six χαλκοῖ. The word is shortened for τριταρτημόριον, which occurs only in Pollux, ix. 65, οἱ δὲ καὶ τριταρτημόριον αὐτοὺς (sc. τοὺς ἐξ χαλκοῦς) ὠνόμαζον ὡς τρία τεταρτημόρια ἔχοντας, and is in turn an abbreviated form of τριτεταρτημόριον.[29] But at first sight the similarity between (τε)ταρτημόριον and τριτημόριον almost inevitably suggests that, if (τε)ταρτημόριον = ¼-obol, τριτημόριον = ⅓-obol. This gave rise to Photius' remark s.v. τριτημόριον (repeated in almost identical terms by Suidas, s.v.) θαυμάζω οὖν ἐγὼ πῶς τεταρτημόριόν εἰσι δύο χαλκοῖ, τριτημόριον δὲ ἔξ· εἰ μὴ ἄρα ἐκεῖνο μὲν κυρίως ὠνομάσθη τέταρτον μέρος τοῦ ὀβολοῦ, τὸ δὲ

---

[29] I cannot find any occurrence of this word, which, however, Schwabacher takes (though misspelling it, as Babelon, τριτηταρτημόριον) as the title of his valuable article in RE vii A 243 f. He does not mention the form τριταρτημόριον, nor does RE give cross-references to his article s.vv. tritartemorion, tritemorion.

τριτημόριον ὡς ἀπὸ τεσσάρων μερῶν ὄντων ἀνὰ δύο χαλκοῦς, τρία ἔχων μέρη, ἐξ χαλκοῦς συνάγει. Occasionally τριτήμορον appears in place of τριτημόριον. Hesychius has an entry ἐκ τριτημόρου· ἐκ τεσσάρων· ἡμιεκτέων, and in the two passages of Philemon quoted by Pollux, ix. 65 f. (see above), the poet uses τριτήμορον to denote ¾-obol.³⁰ In the accounts of the Athenian amphictyons of Delos exhibited on that island we find τριτήμορον Ἀττικόν, Ἀττικὸν τριτήμορον (BCH x. 464 f., ll. 73, 106 ; Rouse, Greek Votive Offerings, 401, wrongly writes τριτημόριον) and in those exhibited at Athens [τριτήμορον Ἀττικόν] can be confidently restored (IG ii². 1636. 30).

See further Babelon, Traité, i. 433, Schwabacher, RE vii A 243 f.

I come finally to the question of the symbols used to denote the obol and its multiples and fractions, and here I confine myself, in accordance with the title of this article, to the available epigraphical material; that afforded by coin-legends receives sufficient attention in the numismatic articles in Babelon, Traité, and RE to which I have already referred.

In the acrophonic numeral system the unit is denoted by I, but in the adaptation of that system for the expression of weights or values, although the unit of reckoning is the drachma, it is the obol, not the drachma, which is indicated by I, the drachma being represented by a differentiated form of I, usually ⊢. Thus HΔΓ⊢⊢III stands for 117 dr. 3 ob., whether as a sum of money or as a weight. A further departure from consistency lies in the fact that, though the perfected acrophonic system used in Attica and in most other states never requires the repetition of the same sign more than four times in succession (e.g. IIII = 4, but Γ = 5), 5 obols is almost invariably expressed by IIIII ; a sixfold repetition is rendered unnecessary by the fact that 6 obols = 1 drachma, so that for IIIIII we write ⊢.

This use of I to represent the obol is found not only in Attica, but also at Hermione, Epidaurus, Andania, Tegea, Dyme, Oropus, Thebes, Thespiae, Acraephia, Delphi, Corcyra, Delos, Ceos, Paros, Naxos, Amorgos, Cos, Samos, Lindus, Imbros, Chalcedon, Teos,

---

³⁰ I do not understand the remark of Pollux (ix. 66) τὸ δὲ παρὰ Φιλήμονι τριτήμορον τεταρτημόριον καλεῖ ἐνίοτε Πλάτων.

and Halicarnassus.[31] It is unnecessary to give references for this usage, normal throughout the Greek world ; the evidence for each of these places can be found by means of the index in *BSA* xxxvii. 258.

In an acrophonic system it might well be expected that the obol should be represented by O, the initial letter of ὀβολός, and such is, in fact, sporadically the case. On an abacus from the Athenian Acropolis and twice on another abacus, found at Eleusis, O follows immediately after ⊢ and denotes the obol (*IG* ii². 2778, 2780), as it also does in inscriptions of Thespiae (*BSA* xxxvii. 244), Boeotian Orchomenus (xviii. 110, xxviii. 143 f.), Thyrrheum (xxviii. 144 f., xxxvii. 247 f.), and Carystus (xviii. 113, xxviii. 145), as well as on the "Darius-vase" (xviii. 124, xxviii. 150). A British Museum fragment from Erythrae has the sign Ō, apparently with the same value (xxviii. 147 f.). The only other obol-sign known to me is the horizontal line —, which occurs as an element in the Erythraean symbol just mentioned and is found by itself at Argos (*BSA* xviii. 102), Nemea (xviii. 103, xxviii. 142), Troezen (xviii. 104 f.), Oropus (xviii. 108), Paros (*IG* xii (5). 186), Eretria (*BSA* xxviii. 145), and Pergamum (xviii. 120, xxviii. 147).

Multiples of the obol are normally represented by the repetition of the obol-sign, but in many places there is a special symbol for three obols (i.e. the half-drachma). This takes the form of T (= τριώβολον) at Andania (*BSA* xxviii. 143, 156), Thespiae (xviii. 109, xxxvii. 244), Thyrrheum (xxviii. 144 f., xxxvii. 247 f.), Naxos (xviii. 113, 116 f.), and Chalcedon (xviii. 120, xxviii. 147), of various signs representing a half (i.e. half-drachma), namely < at Astypalaea (*IG* xii (3). 168. 7), S at Oropus (*BSA* xviii. 108), and Paros (*IG* xii (5). 186) and Ϛ at Eretria (*BSA* xxviii. 145), and perhaps of Υ at Calydon (xxxvii. 247). Teos and Delos occasionally use special signs for five obols ; in the former a small O is placed inside Π (xxviii. 148), in the latter a small I is attached to the under side of the horizontal stroke of Γ (*IG* xi. 224 *A* 10 [258 B.C.], *Inscr. Délos*, 371 *A* 6 [202 or 201 B.C.], 401 *bis B* 2 [190 B.C.], &c.). In a

---

[31] In a third-century inscription (*IG* iv. 526) from the Argive Heraeum I *may* denote the obol (*BSA* xviii. 103), as also in an early fifth-century Corinthian text containing the phrase ζαμία ‖‖‖‖‖ (xxviii. 142, xxxvii. 238).

EPIGRAPHICAL NOTES ON GREEK COINAGE   83

few Delian inscriptions ||| stands not for τρεῖς ὀβολοί but for the single coin, the τριώβολον (*BCH* xv. 151 note 2).[32]

Fractions of the obol may be expressed as multiples of the χαλκοῦς, but in many states there were special symbols for the half- and quarter-obol. The former is normally represented by the sign for a half, whether curved or rectilinear. C is found in Attica (*BSA* xviii. 101, xxxvii. 237 f.), Oropus (xxviii. 143), Delphi (xviii. 107, 111), Thyrrheum (xxviii. 144 f., xxxvii. 247 f.), Paros (xviii. 114), Amorgos (xviii. 117), Imbros (xviii. 119, xxviii. 147), Eretria (xxviii. 145), C and < at Epidaurus (xviii. 103 ff., xxxvii. 238 ff.) and Delos (xviii. 115 f., xxxvii. 250 f.), < at Andania (xxviii. 143, 156) and Erythrae (xxviii. 147 f.) and on the "Darius-vase" (xviii. 124, xxviii. 150), and ∠ at Lindus (xviii. 117). At Boeotian Orchomenus (xviii. 109 f.) and Acraephia (xxxvii. 245) H (= ἡμιωβέλιον) is used, H or < at Thespiae (xviii. 109 f., xxxvii. 244), E at Tegea (xviii. 105 f.), — at Hermione (xviii. 105) and Corcyra (xviii. 112 f.), ⊓ at Troezen (xviii. 104 f.), Γ at Naxos (xviii. 113, 116 f.), and apparently ⊞ at Nemea (xviii. 103, xxviii. 142). The quarter-obol is usually represented by T (= τεταρτη-μόριον, ταρτημόριον), as at Epidaurus, Hermione, Tegea, Acraephia, Delphi, Corcyra, Delos, and Imbros, and on the "Darius-vase"; at Athens and Oropus both T and Ɔ are in use, at Andania >, at Halicarnassus — (xviii. 122), and at Troezen I. Certain other signs are of doubtful value, < or Σ at Nemea, O at Troezen, O and Σ at Pergamum (xviii. 120, xxviii. 147).

From the foregoing summary I have omitted the unique Cyrenean notation, which I have discussed at some length in *BSA* xxxvii. 255 ff.

MARCUS N. TOD

---

[32] In *BSA* xviii. 116 I wrote, with reference to Delos, that "a form ⊩ representing 5/4 obol, *i.e.* |T, is found in *BCH* vi. 6 ff. l. 207". This is wrong; the revised edition of the text given in *Inscr. Délos*, 442 *A* 207 shows that the true reading is not ⊩T but ||||T.

EPIGRAPHICAL NOTES ON GREEK COINAGE: ADDENDA

To recent volumes of the *Numismatic Chronicle* I contributed epigraphical notes on the kollybos (1945, pp. 108 ff.), the chalkous (1946, pp. 47 ff.), and the obolos (1947, pp. 1 ff.), but inscriptions which have been published, or have come to my notice, subsequently call for some additional remarks.

To the examples cited (*N.C.* 1945, pp. 109 f.) for κόλλυβα in the sense of "cakes" or "pastries" we should probably add κόλλυ]βα, restored by Kumanudes in a Spartan *lex sacra* of about the first century A.D. (*I.G.* v (i), 363. 11),[1] while for its second meaning, "agio", "rate of exchange", we may quote ἀ[τέλειαν δὲ εἶναι αὐτῷ ἐπὶ]‖ τῷ κολλύβῳ from an honorary decree of Histria published by Pârvan.[2] The Callimachean fragment in which κόλλυβος is used in the third sense, denoting a coin of trifling value (*N.C.* 1945, p. 111), has now been re-edited by R. Pfeiffer.[3] L. Robert calls attention (*Hellenica* vi, p. 11) to the surname Κολλυβᾶς borne by a magistrate on some Augustan coins of Smyrna and by one of the θεραπευταί whose names were engraved in the first or second century A.D. on a Hellenistic dedication to Sarapis and Isis at Magnesia sub Sipylo, pointing to the use of κολλυβᾶς with the meaning "pastry cook" or "money-changer".

To my paragraph (*N.C.* 1946, p. 55) on the signs used in papyri and ostraka to denote obols and chalkoi I should have added a reference to U. Wilcken's note entitled "Die Chalkussiglen in der griechischen Kursive" (*Hermes*, xxii, pp. 633 ff.).

The ὀβελίσκοι (cf. *N.C.* 1947, p. 1) which figure in fourth-century Attic temple-inventories (e.g. *I.G.* ii², 1426. 12, 1463. 26, 1464. 9) and in a Delian inventory of 235 or 234 B.C. (*Inscr. Délos*, 313 *i* 15, 17) are probably spits, and if in the last of these passages we restore ὀβελίσκου[ς βου]πόρους, we may conclude that the word, though

---

[1] In ll. 13, 16 of this inscription the otherwise unattested word τρώγανα occurs; the reading seems certain, but in view of the frequent use of τρωγάλια (see LS⁹ and add Hsch. *s.v.* κόλλυβα) I am tempted to suggest that the engraver may have misread as Ν the ΛΙ of his copy.

[2] *Dacia*, ii, pp. 205 f., no. 9, ll. 5 f. My attention was called to this passage by J. and L. Robert, *Bull. épigr.* 1948, no. 24.

[3] *Callimachus*, i. 161, fr. 191. 2, *Callimachi fragmenta nuper reperta*, 85.

diminutive in form, does not necessarily indicate a small spit or skewer.[4] A new word ὀβελισκοποιός appears in the sale-lists of the Hermocopidae, dating from 414 or 413 B.C. (*Hesperia*, xxii, p. 271 = *S.E.G.* xiii. 17. 20).

Of my remarks (*N.C.* 1947, pp. 1 f.) on the ὀβελίας ἄρτος and the ὀβελιαφόροι the Athenian Agora has meanwhile provided an interesting illustration in the form of a painting on a polychrome oinochoe of about 400 B.C., depicting two bearded running figures carrying a white object, in all probability a loaf, on a long spit; this was discovered in 1954 and is published by M. Crosby (*Hesperia*, xxiv, pp. 80 f., no. 3, pls. 35 B, 36 A), who calls attention to a similar painting on a phlyax bell-krater of the early fourth century, now in Leningrad (*ibid.* pl. 36 C).[5]

Of the use of ὀβελός in a monetary sense I cited (*N.C.* 1947, p. 3) one Attic example, the [χα]|λκία: καὶ ὀβελ[ὸν ὀφ]λὲν π - - of the "Hekatompedon inscription" (*I.G.* i². 3. 21 f.), but this I now regard as doubtful. The word χαλκία can hardly bear a monetary meaning and its association with ὀβελ[όν suggests that this also refers to a utensil rather than to a coin. A. E. Raubitschek has proposed a new restoration, ὀβελ[ὸς π]λὲν π - - (*S.E.G.* x. 4),[6] but Professor G. Klaffenbach, who at my request has kindly examined the squeeze, reports that this cannot stand because there are five letter-spaces between οβε and λεν, and, even if the colon : had stood in the gap, it would not have occupied a letter-space. So it appears that we must retain ὀφ]λὲν (or perhaps substitute τε]λὲν); true, one obol seems a very trivial penalty (or payment) to prescribe, but we might possibly meet this objection by suggesting ὀβελ[ὸς ὀφ]λὲν (or τε]λὲν) π[έντε - -. Another, and earlier, example of the monetary use of ὀβελός may, however, perhaps be found in the τέταρας ὀβελός of a Marathonian document of the late sixth century (*S.E.G.* x. 2. 13), where the meaning "spits" is highly improbable.[7] The collocation of χαλκίον and

---

[4] Cf. Hdt. ii. 135 ὀβελοὺς βουπόρους σιδηρέους, Eur. *Cyclops*, 302 f. οὐκ ἀμφὶ βουπόροισι πηχθέντας μέλη | ὀβελοῖσι. Of the numerous words ending in -πόρος only βουπόρος suits the present context.

[5] Cf. *Arch. Anz.* 1954, pp. 717 f., fig. 7, 720.

[6] For a photo of part of this inscription see *A.J.A.* lv, pl. 36 B.

[7] For this inscription cf. J. and L. Robert, *Bull. épigr.* 1944, no. 95; W. K. Pritchett, *Cl. Phil.* xlix, p. 42. In a *boustrophedon* text of the late sixth or early fifth century the letters βελ (*S.E.G.* xii. 3 *j* 2) may belong to some part of the

ὀβελός (ὀβολός) recurs in a *lex sacra* of *c.* 445 B.C. from Paeania, Ἀνθεί[ο]|ισι καὶ Πρεροσίοις: ὀβολ|ὸς: χαλκίον (*S.E.G.* x. 38 B 7 ff.),[8] where ὀβολός is apparently an otherwise unexampled spelling of ὀβελός = "spit".

I remarked (*N.C.* 1947, p. 6) on the frequent elision of the short final vowel of δύο and other numerals before ὀβολοί. This solves, I think, a problem raised by a fragmentary inscription of Ceos, which contains several references to sums of money. In l. 6 the majuscule copy of *I.G.* xii (5), 530 gives ....ΤΟΒΟΥΛΟΥ.........., and the transcript, ignoring the initial *T*, - -] ὀβολοὺ[ς δύο(?) - -; but E. Preuner pointed out (*Ath. Mitt.* xlix, p. 135) that Bröndsted's copy shows ΤΟΒΟΛΟΥ, and Hiller von Gaertringen therefore suggested "An πεντ-, ὀκτ-, ἑπτ- οβόλου?" (*I.G.* xii, Suppl., p. 113). None of these words, however, is otherwise attested, and I should much prefer to restore πέν]τ' (or ἐπ]τ', or even ὀκ]τ') ὀβολού[ς - -.[9]

Of Greek parallels to our elliptical expression "two and sixpence" I have cited (*N.C.* 1947, p. 7) examples from Attica, Epidaurus, and Boeotia, and can add one from Delos, ὁλκὴ ἑκατὸν | εἴκοσι ἐξ ὀβολοὶ δύο (*I.G.* xi, 154 B 41 f.), i.e. 126 dr. 2 ob., and in the same inventory we find the double ellipse, comparable to our common phrase "two and six", ὁλκὴ ἑκατὸν τετταράκ[ον]|τα ὀκτὼ τέτταρες (*ibid.* 43 f.), i.e. 148 dr. 4 ob.

Of the forms of words denoting multiples of the obol something more must be said. I recognized (*N.C.* 1947, p. 13) only τριώδελον as the Dorian form of τριώβολον, but J. Papadimitriou, in publishing the opening lines of a fourth-century *lex sacra* discovered in the Epidaurian Asclepieum (*B.C.H.* lxxiii, pp. 366 ff. = *S.E.G.* xi, p. 227, no. 419 *a*), restored in l. 5 τριωδέ[λιον], stating that "la première partie du texte, gravée στοιχηδόν, se laisse aisément restituer"; since, however, the number of letters in the lines restored by him varies

word ὀβελός, but in so fragmentary an inscription its meaning cannot be determined.

[8] In *N.C.* 1947, p. 3, n. 5, I took ὀβολός to be an accusative plural; I now prefer to regard it as a nominative singular.

[9] See *N.C.* 1947, pp. 17 ff. For ὀκτ' ὀβολοί see *ibid.*, pp. 6, 19. Another example of ὀκτὼ 'βολοί is found in *I.G.* ii². 1672. 206 (329/8 B.C.) ἐξ ὀκτὼ 'β[ο]λῶν καὶ ἡμιωβελίου. A further example of elision is afforded by a decree of about 455/4 B.C. regulating the port-dues levied at Sunium (*S.E.G.* x. 10), which has ℏεπ]τ' (or possibly πέν]τ') ὀβολ[ό]ς (l. 18), ℏεπτὰ ‖[ὀβολός (ll. 20 f.), and ℏεπτ' ὀβο[λό]ς (l. 21).

between 21 and 25, we may, I think, assume that here also the form used was τριώδε[λον] and that this line, like the following, contained 21 letters.[10] The same inscription also offers further examples of ὀδελός and ἡμιωδέλιον.

A difficulty is caused by the appearance of a masculine form τριώβολος in several Delian inventories of the second century B.C.—τριώβολοι ΙΙ in *Inscr. Délos*, 1429 B ii 25, τριώβολ[οι] δύο ibid. 24, τριώβο[λοι] in 1443 A ii 63, τρι[ώβολοι ΙΙ] in 1464. 3, [τρι]ώβ[ολοι in 1428 ii 78. Are we to regard τριώβολος as an alternative form of τριώβολον? In answering this question we are hampered by the fact that in the accusative, genitive and dative singular and in the genitive and dative plural τριώβολος and τριώβολον have the same forms. We must, however, bear in mind four facts:

(1) that in the examples of τριώβολοι quoted above the final -οι is preserved only once and is restored in the remaining four places;

(2) that the number of examples, alike in literature and inscriptions, in which the neuter τριώβολον is certain, is very great;[11]

(3) that the masculine form does not appear until shortly before 150 B.C.;

(4) that no trace is found of a masculine form of any other multiple of the obol.

My impression is that τριώβολος is a "freak" form, due either to error or to caprice on the part of the officials who drafted, or of the stonemasons who engraved, the inventories.

Sometimes the word τριώβολον is represented by three obol-signs, ΙΙΙ, as in 'Επιδαύριον ΙΙΙ (*I.G.* xi. 161 A 37), [Αἰγιναῖον ΙΙΙ] (restored in *I.G.* xi. 204. 5 on the basis of τριώβολον Αἰγιναῖον in 203 B 23), Βοιώτιον ΙΙΙ (*Inscr. Délos*, 442 B 193, 443 Bb 117, 444 B 36).[12]

---

[10] At the end of l. 3 I should prefer to restore ὅσ[α] rather than ὅσ[οι], taking πά[ντ]α, rather than τοῖς προθνομένοις, as the antecedent; this would reduce to 24 letters (as in ll. 1, 2) the only 25-letter line.

[11] From Delos we have, for example, *Inscr. Délos*, 296 *b* 49, 313 *d* 3.

[12] These three entries, relating to the years 179–177 B.C., place the Boeotian triobol immediately after the hoard of Orchomenian obols (see below). In earlier years Βοι[ώτιοι ΙΙΙΙ] (*Inscr. Délos*, 367. 20), Βοιώτιοι ΙΙΙΙ (396 B 82) and Βοι]ώτ[ιοι ΙΙΙΙ (399 B 130) occupy this position; I think it likely that in 396 B 82 Βοιώτιοι ΙΙΙΙ has been misread for Βοιώτιον ΙΙΙ, and that Βοιώτιον ΙΙΙ, rather than Βοιώτιοι ΙΙΙΙ, should be restored in the other two passages. See the following footnote.

I pointed out (*N.C.* 1947, p. 5, n. 7) that, though the form ἡμιωβόλιον is found in Pollux, "Suidas", and perhaps Hesychius, it does
not occur in inscriptions with the exception of *I.G.* iv² (1) 110 A 40.
In *I.G.* ii². 1636. 17 [ἐν τοῖς ΙΙΙ ἡμιωβολίοις] is restored, but this appears
to be an error of the editor or the printer, for the Delian inventory of
364 B.C., on which the restoration is based, shows clearly ἡ‖μιωβελίοις
(Michel, *Recueil*, 815. 59 f.).[13]

An interesting illustration of the inefficiency which characterized
the custody of the sacred treasures at Delos[14] is afforded by the successive entries in inventories of the Delian Artemision relating to a
hoard of 410 obols of (presumably Boeotian) Orchomenus. These are
duly registered in 279 (*I.G.* xi. 161 B 19), 278 (162 B 16) and 276 B.C.
(164 A 64, restored). In 274 only 400 are entered (199 B 44), but
this seems to be an error on the part of the hieropoioi or of the
engraver, for in 269 the number is again 410 (203 B 70). In 250, however, only 398 were discovered in the annual stocktaking (287 B 29),
and this figure recurs in a list after 244 B.C. and another after 224 B.C.
(*Inscr. Délos*, 296 B 49, 338 B*b* 13);[15] shortly before 206 B.C. the
number is reduced to 386 (367. 20) and this sinks to 358 in 194, 192,
179, 178, and 177 B.C.[16]

I close these addenda by calling attention to two recent articles
which are of special importance for the study of the obol. In one,
entitled "Tripodi, lebeti, oboli" (*Riv. Fil.* lxxii–lxxiii, pp. 171 ff.),
M. Guarducci discusses the references in archaic inscriptions of
Gortyn and Cnossus to τρίποδες, λέβητες, and ὀβελοί, and their transi-
tion from household utensils to articles with a recognized monetary
value. She also has interesting comments on the spits from the Argive
Heraeum, the Perachora drachma inscription, the iron currency of

---

[13] In ll. 72 f. of this inventory Michel, following Homolle, gives Συμμαχί‖[α]
Μηλία ἀνέθηκε ΙΙΙ, δήλιον Ι καὶ τριτήμορον ἀττικόν, but this fails to specify the mint of
the three obols (or the triobol), while recording those of the obol and the
τριτήμορον (⅔-obol); I should prefer to punctuate ΙΙΙ Δήλιον, Ι (i.e. τριώβολον Δήλιον,
ὀβολὸν καὶ τριτήμορον Ἀττικόν).

[14] For another aspect of the inefficiency of the officials charged with the
custody of the contents of the ancient temples see my remarks in *B.S.A.* xlix,
p. 3.

[15] I cannot but regard the restoration [ΗΗΗ⊢ΔΔΔΓΙΙΙΙ (= 389)] in 338 B*b*
13 as doubtful; if it is correct, it indicates a further drop from 398 to 389.

[16] In *Inscr. Délos*, 1444 A*a* 16 f., dated 141/0 B.C., we find the entry ὀβολοὶ Ι
.. ΔΓ['Ο]ρχομένιοι. If, as seems probable, this refers to the same hoard, the
number of obols had by that time sunk to 215 at most.

Sparta, the ὀβελίσκων δαρχμαί of Chorsiae (*B.C.H.* lxii, pp. 149 ff.), and Rhodopis' iron spits dedicated at Delphi (Hdt. ii. 135), where a fragment of what is claimed as the accompanying votive stele has recently come to light.[17] In the other (*B.C.H.* lxxiii, pp. 177 ff.) J. Pouilloux edits, under the title ὁ ἐπικέφαλος ὀβολός, a new Delphian fragment containing the opening lines of a list of contributions towards the cost of rebuilding the Temple of Apollo, preceded by the names of the archon, three προστατεύοντες, and three ἀργυρολογέοντες. Its main interest lies in the heading τοίδε τῶν Ἀμφικτιόνων | ἤνικαν τοῦ ἐπικεφάλου ‖ ὀβολοῦ τοῦ δευτέρου (ll. 13–15), which affords the first clear evidence that the contributions were reckoned on a capitation basis and leads to a re-examination of the phrases ὁ πρῶτος and ὁ δεύτερος ὀβολός, which are of frequent occurrence in the lists.

MARCUS N. TOD

---

[17] E. Mastrokostas, Γέρας Ἀντωνίου Κεραμοπούλλου (Athens, 1953), pp. 636 ff.

EPIGRAPHICAL NOTES ON GREEK COINAGE[1]

IV. ΔΡΑΧΜΗ

HAVING said something in recent volumes of the *Numismatic Chronicle* about the contribution of inscriptions to the study of the κόλλυβος (1945, 108–16), the χαλκοῦς (1946, 47–62), and the obol (1947, 1–27, 1955, 125–30), I now turn to the drachma. The subject is large and difficult, and the relevant material is abundant and widely scattered. In the present notes I do not claim or attempt to treat it exhaustively,[2] but I hope that their very limitation will be approved by scholars who ἴσασιν ὅσῳ πλέον ἥμισυ παντός.

Ancient authors and lexicographers agree in deriving the noun δραχμή from the verb δράσσομαι and regarding its primary meaning as 'handful',[3] and in this view modern philologists concur,[4] though the ultimate origin of the word is uncertain. With δραχμή the word ὀβελῶν or ὀβολῶν is understood, though not expressed,[5] and the number of 'spits' composing the 'handful' is normally reckoned as six.[6] The word takes various forms. It appears as δραχμή in Ionic,[7] as δραχμά in

Peloponnesian and Island Doric, Boeotian,[1] and Northwestern Greek,[2] as δράχμα in Aeolic,[3] and as δαρχμά in Arcadian (e.g. *Cl. Phil.* 38, 192, *IG* 5 (2), 3 and 6 *passim*) and Elean (e.g. *GDI* 1154, 1155, 1158). In Crete δαρκμά appears at Cnossus (*GDI* 5071. 1, 3) and δαρκνά at Gortyn (e.g. in the Law of Gortyn, i. 9, 33, &c.), but the archaic Cretan alphabet used the form K to represent the sound both of *kappa* and *chi*. The δραχῶν of *GDI* 5492. 47 (Tenos), the δραχάς of *IG* 5 (2). 357. 98 (Stymphalus), the δραχᾶς of *GDI* 1951. 5 (Delphi), and the δράς of *IG* 7. 3077. 6 (Lebadea) are, I believe, engravers' errors and not deliberate contractions.[4] Only once do we meet the diminutive form δραχμίον, which is used in a somewhat disparaging sense,[5] and even this one example is dubious.

LS recognizes two meanings of δραχμή, (1) a weight, and (2) a silver coin worth six obols. To these we may add (3) a sum or value, whether consisting of a single coin or composed of two or more coins of smaller denominations, e.g. a triobol, a diobol, and an obol. Occasionally the use of the same word or symbol to denote a weight and a value may lead to ambiguity, though normally the context serves to determine the meaning.[6] Very often, however, attention is called to the fact that a weight is intended by the addition of a verb, usually ἕλκω or ἄγω,[7] or of a noun, σταθμός or ὁλκή, of which the latter was sometimes used to denote the drachma-weight.[8] Σταθμός is often abbreviated to στα (e.g. *IG* 2². 1492 *passim*) or στα: (e.g. *IG* 2². 1486, 1487. 23) or σταθ: (e.g. *IG* 2². 1412 *passim*), &c., and ὁλκή appears in *BMus. Inscr.* 980. 3, 5 (Cyprian Salamis) in the abbreviated formula Ο∠ρ̄κ̄, Ο∠μ̄η̄. Ὁλκή and ὁλκήν are used indiscriminately in the Delian temple inventories; in *IG* 11. 161 *B* (279 B.C.), for example, we find

---

[1] e.g. *IG* 7. 2420. 23, 24; but see above, p. 1, n. 5.

[2] *IG* 9 (1). 694. 54 (Corcyra) is wrongly cited by van Herwerden, *Lexicon*, s.v. δαρχμά.

[3] *IG* 12 Suppl. 139. 13, 105, *IG* 12 (2). 15. 36.

[4] The Tenian inscription is *IG* 12 (5). 872, which gives δραχμῶν without comment, but the copy in *BMus. Inscr.* 377. 47 and the text in *GDI* loc. cit., with Bechtel's note 'δρα-χ(μ)ῶν: M übergangen', point to the absence of M. In *IG* 7. 3077 the full form δραχμάς occurs *passim*.

[5] Aristeas, *De LXX interpr.* 27 (not 5, as in LS) εἴκοσι δραχμία δοθήσεται. But Wendland's edition gives εἰκοσαδραχμία.

[6] In English the word 'pound' is used both for a weight and for a value, but here we are guided not only by the context, but also by the difference between the two abbreviations of the Latin *libra*, '£' indicating value and 'lb.' weight.

[7] e.g. *Michel* 815. 39 (Delos, 364 B.C.) συναμφότερα δὲ εἵλκυσε ΧΧΔΔΠⲎⲎⲎⲎ, *IG* 2². 1396. 32, 33 σταθμὸν ἄγει, *IG* 7. 3498. 61 (Oropus) ταῦτα ἤγαγον τετράχμα γ′ καὶ [δραχμ]ήν. The participles ἄγων, ἄγουσα, &c., are very frequent in the lists from Didyma (see *Didyma* 2, Index, p. 344).

[8] Galen 19. 775 ἡ δὲ δραχμή, ἡ καὶ ὁλκὴ λεγομένη, ἄγει γράμματα τρία, τουτέστιν ὀβολοὺς ς′. Ὁλκή and σταθμός are frequently used at Didyma: see Rehm's discussion in *Didyma* 2, pp. 251–2.

ὁλκὴ δραχμαί in l. 23, ὁλκὴν δραχμαί in ll. 26, 27, ὁλκὴν δραχμάς in l. 107, ὁλκὴν ἡ πρώτη δραχμάς in l. 30, but ὁλκὴ τῆς πρώτης δραχμαί in l. 33, ὁλκὴ τοῦ χρυσίου δραχμαί... τοῦ ἀργυρίου ὁλκήν in l. 35. In the Athenian lists σταθμός is used, always in the accusative case, sometimes with an added τούτου or τούτων.

The weight is normally recorded with great precision, though the variations in the weight of the same object shown in the inventories of different years indicate some lack of accuracy in the apparatus employed or of care in its use. Sometimes the weights must have been approximate, as is suggested by the added epithet in the phrase ἧς ὁλκὴ δραχμαὶ ἀκριβεῖς Η;[1] we cannot, for instance, believe that all the silver φιάλαι registered in the *catalogi paterarum argentearum* (*IG* 2². 1553–75) weighed precisely 100 drachmae. Sometimes a word is added indicating the weight standard employed: thus at Didyma we find phrases such as φιάλη ... ἐφ' ἧς ἐπιγραφή· ἐπιχώριαι ἐνενήκοντα or φιάλη ἐφ' ἧς ἐπιγραφή· ὁλκὴ Ἀλεξάνδρειαι ἑκατόν (*Didyma*, 471. 6–9), φιάλη ἐ]πιγραφὴν ἔχουσα 'Ροδίας μὲν [ὀγδοήκοντα, Ἀλεξαν]δρε[ί]ας δὲ ἑξήκοντα δύο (ibid. 464. 11–12), ὁλκὴν ἄγουσα Ἀλεξανδρείου δραχμάς (ibid. 433. 8), and στα]θμὸν ἄγει συμμαχι[κοῦ δραχμάς (ibid. 437. 6–7).[2]

The definition of the drachma as 'a silver coin worth six obols', though true in general, needs some modification. As regards the number of obols, see p. 1, n. 6, and the reference to 'silver' leaves out of account some exceptional cases. Thus we find an entry χρυσᾶς: ⊢⊢: in *IG* 2². 1388. 69 (Athens, 398–397 B.C.), χρυσαῖ δραχμαί: ⊢⊢: in an inventory of the Athenian Asclepieum, *IG* 2². 1533. 21 (339–338 B.C.), δραχμὰ χρυσέα in a Delphian account of the last quarter of the fourth century B.C. (*Delphes* 3 (5). 80. 15), and Καρυστία ⊢ χρυσῆ in a Delian inventory of 179 B.C. (*ID* 442 *B* 189; cf. *ENG* 157). References to bronze drachmae are numerous both in inscriptions and in papyri (e.g. *PSI* 571. 16, 599. 9). In *IG* 7. 2426 (Thebes, 150–100 B.C.), for example, bronze drachmae are repeatedly named, showing that these circulated side by side with silver drachmae and were of equal value; thus in ll. 18–19 we find λοιπὸν | ⌐ΗΔΔ⊢· ἐν τούτωι ἀργυρίου ⌐Η καὶ χαλκοῦ ΔΔ⊢ (cf. also *IG* 12 (3). 253. 13). Nor must we overlook the καττιτερίνη (sc. δραχμή) found in the Delian inventories between 'Ροδίας ἕξ and ἡμιρόδια τέτταρα,[3] in which Robert sees a Rhodian drachma, a 'monnaie fourrée', 'dont la pellicule

---

[1] *ID* 1432 *Ba* i 16.
[2] See Rehm, *Didyma* 2, pp. 262–4. Didyma 464, 471 = *Michel* 837, 838.
[3] *ID* 1442 *B* 52.

d'argent a disparu et dont il ne reste que l'âme en étain' (*ENG* 164–5).

I am not convinced by this explanation, for I doubt whether anything deserving the name of a Rhodian drachma would consist of a basis of tin overlaid with silver, so badly plated that the silver had entirely disappeared, and I am struck by the frequency with which temple inventories call attention to the difference between the surface and the interior of an object by the use of terms such as ὑπάργυρος, ὑπόχαλκος, κίβδηλος, or, on the other hand, ἐπάργυρος, ἐπίχρυσος, κατάχρυσος.[1] I would rather suggest that the donor, seeing the countless array of silver drachmas in the temple treasuries and wishing to offer a more original and striking gift, made for this purpose a tin drachma, possibly of the Rhodian type, with no intention that it should be used as a coin.[2] More ambitious was the dedicator of the golden tetradrachm which appears in the inventories of the Parthenon from 422–421 B.C. onwards.[3] Normally, however, the drachma is a silver coin, and in innumerable instances the word ἀργυρίου (never ἀργυραῖ)[4] precedes or follows δραχμαί, sometimes accompanied by a word indicating their source or nature, e.g. δραχμῶν τοῦ Ῥοδίου ἀργυρίου (*IG* 12 (5). 817. 5; Tenos, ii B.C.), ἀργυρίου Ἀττικοῦ δραχμάς (*IG* 7. 2710. 5; Acraephia), ἀργυρίου συμμαχικοῦ δραχμῶν (*IG* 7. 2426. 16; Thebes, ii B.C.), ἀργυρίου Ἀλεξανδρείου δραχμάς (*OGI* 326. 23; Teos). Even in the absence of ἀργυρίου we may safely assume that silver is in question unless there is some indication to the contrary.

In states where the drachma, rather than the stater, is the unit of reckoning, the mina is usually ignored and the count in drachmae is continued until the talent is reached, and often far beyond that point; thus we have, e.g. ἑξακισχιλίας δραχμάς (*SIG* 1003. 24; cf. *ID* 499. 14, 1401c 12, 17), δραχμὰς ἐνακισχιλίας (*OGI* 751. 6, 14), μυρίας δραχμάς (*IG* 4² (1). 76. 15), δραχμὰς ἑξακισμυρίας (*IG* 12 (9). 236. 58), [δραχμῶν μ]υριάδας δέκα (*IGRom* 4. 316. 14), and even μυριάδες Δ Δ Δ Γ [δ]ραχμα[ί], i.e. 350,000 drachmae[5] (*ID* 465c 22).

In inscriptions, and especially in inventories of temple treasures, such as those of Athens, Delos, Didyma, and elsewhere, drachmae

---

[1] e.g. *IG* 1². 386. 7 ὑπ]άργυρα ἐπίχρυσ[α, 283. 132 ἔλο δύο ηυπαργύρο κατ[αχρύσο (a certain restoration), 2². 1425. 70 κρατὴρ ἐπίτηκτος ἐπίχρυσος ὑπάργυρος.
[2] I agree with Robert, 'Je ne crois pas qu'il soit possible d'y voir de véritables monnaies d'étain, comme on l'a cru' (*ENG* 164, n. 5).
[3] *IG* 1². 280 ff., no. 50. Cf. below, p. 13, n. 3.
[4] The only exception known to me is *IG* 1². 310. 112–13 Χῖα[ι δραχμαί] | ἀργυρ[αῖ]: but δραχμαί is not a certain restoration (it might, e.g., be φιάλαι, as in ll. 199, 210), and even if it is correct, ἀργυρ[αῖ] should perhaps be ἀργυρ[ίο].
[5] For further examples see *BSA* 37, 250.

are often accompanied by adjectives or quasi-adjectival phrases, which add precision to the entries in which they occur. These relate chiefly to the following points:

(a) The number of drachmae in question, expressed in words or in numerals, whether acrophonic or alphabetic. The word δραχμαί precedes or follows the number, and is often represented by a symbol (see below, pp. 20–24). A single drachma is normally expressed by the singular δραχμή, but occasionally μία is added, as in OGI 674. 25, 31 (Coptus) δραχμὴν μίαν, ID 461 Bb 49 (169 B.C.) πλινθοφόρος μία.

(b) The metal of which the coin is composed. Of this I have already spoken.

(c) The state under whose authority it was issued. This may be indicated by the epithet ἐπιχώριος, as in a decree of Ithaca found at Magnesia on the Maeander, SIG 558. 20 δραχμὰς ἐπιχωρίας δεκαπέντε,[1] or by ἡμεδαπός, found in several Attic inscriptions relative to coinage, but normally a local adjective is used: thus in a fragmentary Tenian inscription we find (δραχμὰς) Τηνίας, Ἀχαϊκ[άς] and Μηλίας (IG 12 (5). 878. 2, 5, 6), in a Delian inventory of 364 B.C. Δήλιαι δραχμαὶ ⊢⊢² and Σύριαι δραχμαὶ Γ (Michel 815. 100, 105), and in an Eleusinian record of 329–328 B.C. δραχμὴ Χαλκιδική (IG 2². 1672. 300). Among the many other examples found in the Delian lists are the (δραχμὴ) Λακωνική of ID 1444 Aa 18, the Σικυωνία ⊢ of ID 442 B 204, 444 B 47, and the δραχμὴ Ἀπολλωνιατι[κή (of Apollonia in Illyria) of ID 1422. 14.[3] At Didyma Μιλήσιαι, with or without δραχμαί, occur frequently, but always as units of weight, e.g. Didyma 446. 12 (225–224 B.C.) ὁλκὴ ἑκάστης Μιλήσιαι ἑκατόν. Instead of a feminine adjective agreeing with δραχμαί we often find a neuter adjective in the genitive agreeing with ἀργυρίου or νομίσματος,[4] either expressed (see above, p. 4) or understood, as, for example, in Αἰγιναίου δραχμὰς πέντε, Κορινθίου δραχμὰς τ[ρεῖς], Ἀττικοῦ δραχμάν (BCH 66–67, 102).[5]

Of these local coinages three are outstanding in importance and in the frequency of their appearance in inscriptions—the Attic, the

---

[1] The ἐπιχώριαι (sc. δραχμαί) of Didyma 471. 7 refer to weight, not to value.

[2] In such cases the number of drachmae is sometimes, as here, expressed by drachmasigns even when the word δραχμαί precedes, sometimes by pure numbers, as in ID 1442 B 53 'Ροδίας ||||, IG 7. 3171. 52 δρα. |||.

[3] For Καρυστία ⊢ χρυσῆ see above, p. 3; for Χῖα[ι δραχμαί] see p. 4, n. 4. In IG 4. 752. 10 (Troezen, ii B.C.) we have δραχμὰς διακοσίας ἂν Τροζάνιοι νομίζοντι (cf. IG 4² (1). 77. 16), in ID 1443 A i 150 Ἐφεσίας (δραχμάς).

[4] See IG 12 (9). 207. 21 (Eretria, c. 294–288 B.C.), 12 Suppl. 193. 10.

[5] Cf. Delphes 3 (5) 9 (= SIG 240 L) passim. In IG 4² (1). 97. 21 (Epidaurus, iii B.C.) δραχμὰς Ἀργολικοὺς (!) δύο I should prefer to write Ἀργολικοῦ{ς}, especially as we find [Ἀργολ]ικοῦ δραχμὰς πέντε in l. 36.

Aeginetan, and the Rhodian. Δραχμαὶ Ἀττικαί, or simply Ἀττικαί,[1] occur over a long period and a wide area, and their popularity was attested, and doubtless enhanced, by the Delphian recognition of the Attic tetradrachm (below, p. 14). Outside Attica we find them, e.g. in Delian treasure-lists (*Michel* 815. 57, 67, 72, 95, *ID* 442 *B* 190, 1444 *Aa* 16, &c.) and in an Epidaurian subscription list of the third century B.C. (*IG* 4² (1). 97. 24, 39, 42), and an Ἀττική is the fee paid to the bath-attendant at Epidaurus by a patient from Mylasa in the second or third century A.D. (ibid. 126. 13 = *SIG* 1170. 13). Byzantium contributed to the cost of the Sacred War, c. 355–351 B.C., 584 Lampsacene gold staters and ἀργυρίω Ἀτ[τικῶ δρα]|χμὰς δεκαέξ (*IG* 7. 2418. 9–11, 20–21), and a letter of Antoninus Pius, sent to a Macedonian city[2] in A.D. 158, directs that every βουλευτής shall pay πεντακοσίας Ἀττικάς as a *summa honoraria* (*SEG* 14. 479. 10). In many cities of Asia Minor, some important and others remote and insignificant, and in Palmyra (*IGRom*. 3. 1047. 8), Ἀττικαὶ (δραχμαί) appear in the Imperial period, chiefly in records of benefactions or as defining penalties imposed for tomb-violation.[3] Two Bithynian epigrams of the second or third century A.D. name in iambic verse the fine for violation as Ἀττικὰς τρισχειλίας (Peek, *Griech. Vers-Inschriften*, 1112. 18, from Prusias ad Hypium) and Ἀττικὰς δισχιλίας (ibid. 1946. 15, from Nicaea). Josephus' words τοῦ Τυρίου νομίσματος, ὃ τέσσαρας Ἀττικὰς δύναται (*BJ* 2. 21, 2) suggest that in Palestine the Attic drachma was generally recognized as the unit of value.[4] The Aeginetan drachma, heavier than the Attic,[5] appears very often in Delphian records and also in a third-century law of Stymphalus (*IG* 5 (2). 357. 51, 98, 139), and the text of a financial transaction between Thespiae and Athens in the late third century B.C. contains references to

[1] Frequently misspelt Ἀτικαί. At Epidaurus we have Ἀθικαὶ δραχμαί in *IG* 4² (1). 102. 106 (400–350 B.C.), Ἀτθικοῦ ibid. 104. 9. 'Attic' drachmae may, however, denote drachmae of the Attic standard, not necessarily struck at Athens. In the early Empire, when the Athenian mint issued only bronze coins, the 'Attic' drachma was equated with the Roman denarius.

[2] D. Detchev, the first editor, suggested that the city may be Alexandropolis, but J. and L. Robert favour Parthicopolis (*REG* 61. 169 no. 112, 69. 138 no. 159). See below, p. 21, n. 4.

[3] For some examples see *IGRom*. 4, 739 *s.v.* ἀττική.

[4] See further Hultsch, *RE* 5, 1616–18.

[5] Cf. Pollux 9. 76 ἀλλὰ μὴν τὴν μὲν Αἰγιναίαν δραχμὴν μείζω τῆς Ἀττικῆς οὖσαν (δέκα γὰρ ὀβολοὺς Ἀττικοὺς ἴσχυεν) Ἀθηναῖοι παχεῖαν δραχμὴν ἐκάλουν, μίσει τῶν Αἰγινητῶν Αἰγιναίαν καλεῖν μὴ θέλοντες. For another explanation of the phrase παχεῖα δραχμή see above, p. 1, n. 6. Dr. Robinson holds that 'the gold and silver drachma always contained six obols of its own standard. When another figure is given, it is because the coins, drachms of one standard and obols of another, were circulating side by side, e.g. in Attica, Attic and Aeginetic . . ., or in south Italy, Achaean of Kroton, Sybaris, etc., and Euboic-Chalkidian of Rhegion, Zankle, etc.'

Aeginetan drachmas (*IG* 7. 1737. 5, 10). The alliance of Athens, Argos, Elis, and Mantinea in 420 B.C. prescribes δραχμὴν Αἰγιναίαν as the daily pay due in certain circumstances to a ἱππεύς (*IG* 1². 86. 24, restored from Thuc. 5. 47, 6), and an Αἰγιναία ⊢ occurs in the Delian inventories (*ID* 442 *B* 203, 444 *B* 47). These also contain a number of entries[1] relating to Rhodian drachmae, sometimes called simply ʽΡόδιαι (e.g. *ID* 1442 *B* 52), and a decree of the Νησιῶται found at Tenos refers to the rapacity of the corn-dealers [ἀντὶ ἑκα||τ]ὸν δραχμῶν τοῦ ʽΡοδίου ἀργυρίου οὐκ [ἔλαττον ἀπαιτούντων]‖ ἑκατὸν καὶ πέντε δραχμῶν (*IG* 12 (5). 817. 4–6; early ii B.C.). ʽΡόδιαι (δραχμαί) appear as units of weight in *Didyma* 431. 6 (272–271 B.C.) ὁλκὴ ʽΡόδιαι δραχμαὶ ἑκατὸ[ν] μία and 463. 34; in 464. 11–13 (177–176 B.C.) we find a [φιάλη ἐ]πιγρα-φὴν ἔχουσα ʽΡοδίας μὲν [ὀγδοήκοντα,[2] | Ἀλεξαν]δρε[ί]ας δὲ ἑξήκοντα δύο. An interesting glimpse of the impact of Roman currency on Greek coinage is afforded by an inscription of Cibyra honouring a bene-factor who had given 400,000 Rhodian drachmae to defray in per-petuity the expense of the γυμνασιαρχία; this contains the words τοῦ ʽΡωμαϊκοῦ δηναρίου ἰσχύοντος ἀσσάρια δεκαέξ· | ἡ ʽΡοδία δραχμὴ τούτου τοῦ δηναρίου ἰσχύει ἐν Κιβύρᾳ | ἀσσάρια δέκα, ἐν ᾗ δραχμῇ ʽΡοδίᾳ δέδοται ἡ δωρεά (*IG Rom.* 4. 915. 6, 12–14). Another honorary inscription of the same city records a gift of 54,000 and a loan of 100,000 Rhodian drachmae (ibid. 914. 8–9).[3]

(*d*) Drachmae named after a ruler or dynasty.[4] Among these the commonest are the Ἀλεξάνδρειαι (or Ἀλεξάνδρειοι) δραχμαί, restored in a fragmentary list of gifts for the rebuilding of Thebes towards the end of the fourth century B.C. (*IG* 7. 2419 i 15, ii 4 = *SIG* 337. 15, 20) and in a Chian decree of about the same date (*Rev. Phil.* 23 (1949), 10, ll. 12–13). They recur frequently in the third century, e.g. at Epidaurus in a donation-list and a penalty-record (*IG* 4² (1). 97. 3, 14, &c., 98. 7–8, 11–12), in an inventory of the Oropian Amphiaraion (*IG* 7. 303. 97–98 = *Michel* 827 *B* 45–46), in honorary decrees of Ios (*IG* 12 (5). 1010. 1) and of Nacrasa in Lydia (*OGI* 268. 12), and in Delian inventories (e.g. *ID* 442 *B* 14, 190). In the second century I mention only the ἀργυρίου Ἀλεξανδρείου δραχμὰς μυρίας καὶ πεντακοσίας given to the guild of Attalists at Teos (*OGI* 326. 23), the gift of 18,000 Alexandrine drachmae made to Delphi by Attalus II of Pergamum

---

[1] e.g. *IG* 11. 203 *B* 40 (269 B.C.), 287 *B* 47 (250 B.C.), *ID* 442 *B* 204 (179 B.C.).
[2] Haussoullier's restoration [ὀγδοήκοντα] is not admitted to Rehm's text.
[3] For the Aeginetan drachma cf. Hultsch, *RE* 5, 1615–16; for the Rhodian, ibid. 1619–20.
[4] Cf. Hultsch, *RE* 5, 1618–19; for tetradrachms of this class see below, pp. 14–15.

(*SIG* 672. 8), and decrees of Methymna and Eresus exhibited at Miletus (*IG* 12 Suppl. 139. 13, 104).[1] An Eretrian law of the early third century B.C. speaks of νομίσματος Δημητριείου δραχμὰς ἑξακοσίας (*IG* 12 (9). 207. 21), issued by Demetrius Poliorcetes, and a Δημητρίειος δραχμή occurs in a decree of Gonnus found at Magnesia on the Maeander (*Inscr. Magn.* 33. 20; early ii B.C.). Δραχμαὶ Πτολεμαϊκαί are mentioned in a third-century decree of an unknown city, published at Delos (*IG* 11. 1041. 14–15), and in a letter addressed to Thera by Ptolemy Euergetes in 229 B.C. (*IG* 12 (3). 327. 13–14; cf. p. 230) Πτολεμαϊκὰς (δραχμὰς) ρια', where the drachma-symbol ⱶ was at first taken to be Υ, so that the text appeared as Πτολεμαϊκὰ Σύρια. In Delian inventories we find Φιλίππειον ⱶ (*ID* 1442 *B* 50; cf. *ENG* 163, n. 2), Φιλιππείους δραχμὰς ⱶⱶⱶ (*ID* 1443 *A* i 149), Φιλιππείους τρεῖς (*ID* 1449 *Aab* ii 23), Φιλιππείους δραχμὰς τρεῖς (*ID* 1450 *A* 102),[2] and Περσικὴν δραχμήν (ibid. 112), while Ἀτταλικαὶ δραχμαί[3] are restored in two inscriptions of Pergamum, *IGRom*. 4. 316. 13–14 Ἀττ[αλικῶν | δραχμῶν μ]υριάδας δέκα and 473. 13–14 Ἀττα|[λικὰς μυριάδ]ας δέκα.[4]

(*e*) Some drachmae bear descriptive epithets ending in -φόρος, indicating the emblems stamped on their reverse. These are found chiefly in Delian accounts and inventories of the second century B.C., and some of them are discussed in two masterly chapters (III, VI) of Robert's *Études de numismatique grecque*. Δραχμαὶ στεφανηφόροι,[5] or στεφανηφόρου,[6] or τοῦ στεφανηφόρου[7] occur in a number of Attic and Delian inscriptions, and Robert proves conclusively (pp. 105–35) that these have no connexion with the Attic ἥρως Στεφανηφόρος and are not merely popular expressions, but official designations of Attic drachmae of the 'New Style', inaugurated in, or a little before, 180–179 B.C.,[8] bearing an olive-wreath round the edge of the reverse; thus στεφανηφόρου is not a noun, but, like στεφανηφόρος, an adjective with which ἀργυρίου is understood.[9] He also discusses and identifies

[1] For the first century B.C. see a tribal decree from Mylasa, F. Sokolowski, *Lois sacrées de l'Asie mineure*, 62. 5, 8 (= *Michel* 725. 10, 16). Appian says ἔχει δὲ τὸ Εὐβοϊκὸν τάλαντον Ἀλεξανδρείους δραχμὰς ἑπτακισχιλίας (*Sic*. 2).
[2] *ENG* 163, n. 2.
[3] Hultsch, *RE* 5, 1618–19.
[4] Since μυριάς is a noun, I should prefer to restore Ἀττα|[λικῶν (sc. δραχμῶν) here, but in *IGRom*. 4. 914. 8–9 we find δέκα | μυρ[ι]άδας ['Ρ]οδίας.
[5] For Delian examples see *ENG* 124–5, 129–30.
[6] For Delian examples see *ENG* 123–4, for Attic, 116–17.
[7] *IG* 2². 1013. 33, *ID* 1442 *B* 74.
[8] A. R. Bellinger, *Hesperia*, Suppl. 8, 12, approved by Robert, *ENG* 134–5.
[9] Cf. *ID* 1415. 12 ἀργυρίου Ἀττικοῦ στεφανηφόρου δραχμάς. A third-century decree of Anaphe has ἀργυρίου ἐ[κ στε|φα]νοφόρου δραχ[μᾶν - - (*IG* 12 (3). 254. 32–33).

the Tenian δραχμὴ βοτρυοφόρος,[1] the Rhodian πλινθοφόροι,[2] and the Delian δραχμαὶ φοινικοφόροι,[3] interprets the κρατηροφόροι (or -φόρα) as Naxian drachmae or didrachms,[4] calls attention (*ENG* 177) to a δραχμὴ τριποδηφόρος, and examines (*ENG* 150–2) the Lycian κιθαρηφόροι attested by epitaphs of Myra and Arneae.[5] All these epithets, Robert emphasizes (*ENG* 176–8), are official designations of the coins in question and not just popular nicknames,[6] while the epithet ἱερός, frequently applied to money, indicates merely that it is the property of some deity, not that it belongs to some special issue (*ENG* 136–9).[7]

The adjective δραχμαῖος appears without context in Ar. *Fr.* 425; in Plato, *Cratylus* 384 B τὴν δραχμιαίαν ἐπίδειξιν, it refers to a tutorial fee, and in Arist. *Pol.* 1300[b] 33 συναλλαγμάτων ὅσα δραχμιαῖα to value. Pollux 9. 60 says τὸ δραχμῆς ἄξιον δραχμιαῖον, and such is its meaning in Athen. 6. 274 D ὄρνιθας ὠνεῖτο δραχμιαίους, but in Archigenes, quoted by Galen 12. 876 δραχμιαίους τροχίσκους, the reference is to weight. Most frequently, however, the word occurs in phrases relating to the rate of interest. Thus in *IG* 12 (5). 860. 25 (Tenos, i B.C.) we find δραχμιαῖον τόκον ἐξ εὐθυτοκίας, in *BMus. Inscr.* 481*, 486–7 (Ephesus, A.D. 105) τελέσει τόκον | ... δραχμιαῖον καθ᾽ ἕκαστον ἐ[νιαυτόν], and in *IGRom.* 4. 788. 15 (= *MAMA* 6. 180 ii 15; Apamea, c. A.D. 160) τόκον δραχμιαῖον, while in papyri such phrases are common,[8] sometimes more exactly defined, as in *Sammelb.* 4370. 12 (A.D. 228–9) τόκου δραχμιαίου ἑκάστης μνᾶς | κατὰ μῆνα ἕκαστον,[9] i.e. 12 per cent. Variant forms of the adjective are δραχμαῖος and δραχμήϊος, both denoting weight, which are found only in Nicander, *Theriaca* 519, 604.

I pass now to a rapid survey of the multiples of the drachma, with special reference to the epigraphical evidence.

---

[1] *ENG* 165–6 (examples on p. 165, nn. 3, 4).
[2] *ENG* 166–76 (examples on pp. 167–9).
[3] *ENG* 147–56 (examples on p. 147, n. 6).
[4] *ENG* 160–2 (examples on p. 160, n. 2).
[5] *Ath. Mitt.* 14. 413, *TAM* 2. 779. 2; cf. Regling, *RE* 11, 528–9. The reading δραχμ]ὰς λεοντοφόρους in P. Roussel, *Délos colonie athénienne* 167, has been corrected to δραχμ]ὰς πλιντοφόρους (*ENG* 169). For tetradrachms with epithets in -φόρος see below, p. 15.
[6] The drachma-sign is used jocularly in an inscription from the temple of Petosiris near Hermopolis Magna, in which an iambic epigram (*SEG* 8. 624 = Peek, *Griech. Vers-Inschriften* 1176) is followed by the words κεφάλαιον τούτων τῶν ἰαμβείων | εἰς ἀργύριον [sic] λόγον ⊦,ητογ′ = (*SEG* 8. 625); the numerical values of the letters composing the epigram amount to 8373. Whether the ⊦⊦ in a Tegean ephebe-list (*SEG* 11. 1058) embodies a joke I cannot say.
[7] An epithet occasionally applied to currency is συμμαχικός, as in *IG* 5 (2). 345. 21 (Arcadian Orchomenus), 7. 1743 (Thespiae), 2426 (Thebes), *ID* 1443 *A* i 150, Didyma 434–7.
[8] e.g. *BGU* 1038. 20, *Sammelb.* 5168. 5, 5343. 34.
[9] The same phrase is restored in *POxy.* 1473. 4 (A.D. 201).

2. The comparatively rare appearance of the δίδραχμον[1] in inscriptions is due in part to the fact that in some states, e.g. at Delphi, two drachmae were normally expressed as one stater, and that in the Euboic–Attic standard the didrachm was comparatively seldom struck. Where it does occur, we cannot always determine whether it refers to a single didrachm or to a sum of money of that value. Pollux 9. 60 mentions the 2-drachma piece in his list of coins, and in the Delian temple-inventories we find a δίδραχμον of unspecified mint,[2] a Μήλιον δίδραχμον,[3] a δίδραχμον Φιλίππειον,[4] and a [δί]δ[ρ]αχμον Ἀντιόχ[ειον].[5] The didrachm is also mentioned in Arist. *Ath.* 10. 2 (not 10. 7, as in LS) ἦν δ' ὁ ἀρχαῖος χαρακτὴρ δίδραχμον, in Hsch. παχείᾳ δραχμῇ· τὸ δίδραχμον, Ἀχαῖος,[6] and in *EM* ἑκατόμβη· βοιὸν δὲ λέγουσιν εἶναι σταθμίον τι, ἢ τὴν βοὸς τιμήν, ἢ τὸ δίδραχμον, βοῦν ἔχον ἐπίσημον. Elsewhere Hesychius explains δίδραχμον by συντέλεσις, εἰσφορά, λειτουργία, i.e. a recurrent contribution, whether voluntary or compulsory, and, though it is probable that payment was normally made by a simple didrachm, we need not doubt that the obligation could be met by the payment of 2 drachmae, or of smaller coins amounting to the same sum. An Athenian decree of the period of the Archidamian War (*IG* 1². 79), when no Athenian didrachms were in circulation, orders ἱππεῖς to pay a δ[ίδρ]αχμ[ο]ν, hoplites a drachma, and τοξόται 3 obols out of their pay for the cult of Apollo.[7] Better known are the half-shekel (δίδραχμον) paid by Jews to the Temple treasury at Jerusalem,[8] and, after the destruction of the Temple, to that of Juppiter Capitolinus,[9] and the poll-tax levied by the Romans in Palestine in the time of our Lord.[10] Δίδραχμον was also used for a weight (not in LS), as in Hsch. δίδραχμον· τὸ τέταρτον τῆς οὐγκίας, and δραχμὴ χρυσίου· ὁλκὴ νομίσματος, εἰς ἀργυρίου λόγον διδράχμων ε'. The adjective δίδραχμος refers to money in [Thuc.] 3. 17, where δίδραχμοι ὁπλῖται are those who receive 2 drachmae daily, in Arist. *Oec.* 1353ᵃ17

---

[1] Babelon 419–21; Hultsch, *RE* 5, 433–6; *Wörterbuch* 139. In the manuscripts of the lexicographers the χ frequently becomes γ or drops out altogether.

[2] *ID* 442 *B* 203 (179 B.C.), 1432 *Bb* i 27 (153–152 B.C.).

[3] *ID* 399 *B* 144 (192 B.C.), 444 *B* 47, 1444 *Aa* 18.

[4] *ID* 1449 *Aab* ii 11, 1450 *A* 96.

[5] *ID* 298 *A* 36 (240 B.C.).

[6] A different interpretation of παχεῖα δραχμή is given in Hsch. s.v. λεπτὰς καὶ παχείας where the λεπτή is said to contain 6 obols and the παχεῖα more than 6.

[7] Cf. R. Schlaifer, *Harv. Stud.* 51, 235–6; W. S. Ferguson, *Hesperia*, Suppl. 8, 143–4.

[8] LXX *Ge.* 20. 16, *Ex.* 30. 13 (κατὰ τὸ δίδραχμον τὸ ἅγιον· εἴκοσι ὀβολοὶ τὸ δίδραχμον), *Le.* 27. 25, *Nu.* 3. 47, &c.

[9] Dio Cass. 66. 7 δίδραχμον ἐτάχθη τοὺς τὰ πάτρια αὐτῶν ἔθη περιστέλλοντας τῷ Καπιτωλίῳ Διὶ κατ' ἔτος ἀποφέρειν.

[10] *Ev. Matt.* 17. 24 οἱ τὰ δίδραχμα λαμβάνοντες . . . τελεῖ τὰ δίδραχμα.

τὸν μόλιβδον παραλαμβάνειν δίδραχμον, 'at the price of 2 drachmae', and in a number of inscriptions and papyri referring to δίδραχμος τόκος (or δίδραχμοι τόκοι), 'interest at 24% per annum'. Among these are *IG* 5 (1) 1146. 38 (Gythium, i B.C.,) 5 (2) 357. 140 (Stymphalus), *Chron. d'Ég.* 25. 279 (Egyptian ostrakon, 124 B.C.), and *BGU* 1126. 17 (8 B.C.); in all these cases the word is written in full and its form is assured. In *PHamb.* 28. 5 (ii B.C.) P. M. Meyer writes τ[ό]κων (διδραχμαίων), but, since διδραχμαῖος is otherwise unattested and διδραχμιαῖος is not, so far as I know, used in this context, I should prefer to write in the Hamburg papyrus (διδράχμων).[1] Διδραχμιαῖος is cited by Pollux 4. 165 from Critias, but he gives no context and we cannot tell whether it refers to weight or, as is more probable, to value. Διδραχμία is used of a purchase-tax of 10 per cent. due to the god Σοῦχος (Wilcken, *Einl.* 172), which *BGU* 748 iii 5 (not 741 iii 3, as in LS) calls τὴν διδραχμία(ν) τοῦ Σούχου and to which *PTeb.* 281. 9 (125 B.C.) refers in the words τοῦ ἐξειληφότος τὴν εἰς τὸ ἱερὸν καθή-κουσαν δίδοσθαι διδραχμίαν τῶν κ′ (δραχμῶν), ἥ ἐστιν δεκάτη, 'the tax of 2 drachmae upon each 20, making ¹⁄₁₀'. In an Athenian decree of c. 430 B.C., regulating the cult of Bendis, W. S. Ferguson restored [οἱ δὲ πολεταὶ ἀπομισθοσάντον τὲν τῆι Βενδῖδι δυοδραχμί]αν,[2] but, as this last word occurs nowhere else, I suggest τὲν τῆι Βενδῖδι (or τῆς Βενδῖδος) διδραχμί]αν. A problem is presented by the verse Μήου ἀπὸ ῥίζης ὁλκὴν διδραχμίαν ὀρύξας, quoted from Eudemus in Galen 14. 185; is διδραχμίαν, which here clearly indicates weight and not value, a noun in apposition to ὁλκήν, or is it an adjective agreeing with ὁλκήν, derived from an unattested *διδράχμιος, or should we perhaps emend to διδραχμαίαν, so lessening, though not eliminating, the metrical irregularity?

Two further possible, but doubtful, appearances of the didrachm may be noted. In *Sammelbuch* 5815 we have an ostrakon bearing a tax receipt dated A.D. 77, Δημᾶς Σίμωνο(ς) ΔΙΛ, and Preisigke suggested that the last three letters might stand for διδ(ράχμον) and refer to the Jewish tax. In the longest and best known of Cyprian syllabic inscriptions, which records the honours granted by Salamis c. 450 B.C. to the doctor Onasilus and his family, the signs ΙΙ *ti-e* occur in ll. 16, 26 and are interpreted by Deecke (*GDI* 60), Solmsen–Fraenkel (*IGDial.*[4] 6), and others as β′ δί(δραχμα) Ἠ(δάλια) or Ἠ(δαλιακά), but K. Meister (*IF* 18. 176) argued in favour of δί(μναια) and E. Schwyzer (*DGE* 679)

[1] Other possible references to the τόκος δίδραχμος occur in *PSI* 604. 2, 608. 7, and 1311. 29.
[2] *Hesperia*, Suppl. 8, 134; cf. *SEG* 10. 64 *b* 13.

left the question open. Another possibility would be to regard the *e* as an abbreviation of ἐπιχώρια.[1]

3. The noun τρίδραχμον[2] is rare, and coins bearing that name are by no means frequent, though the Corinthian stater and most of the South Italian νόμοι of the Achaean standard are in fact tridrachms. Pollux 6. 165 cites τρίδραχμον among miscellaneous compounds of τρι-, and it is uncertain whether he had in mind a coin, a value, or a weight; in 9. 60 he mentions it as a coin. The Delian inventory of 364 B.C. includes τρίδραχμα Μαρωνιτικά ‖ (*Michel* 815. 62), and this item is restored in the surviving fragment of the same document exhibited in Athens (*IG* 2². 1636. 19),[3] while in a list of dedications at the Oropian Amphiaraion, dated c. 240 B.C., we find a large number of entries such as Κλεονόης ⊦⊦⊦ (*IG* 7. 303. 76), which refer to dedications consisting of a single tridrachm or of three separate drachmae.[4] For the adjective τρίδραχμος LS cites Ar. *Pax* 1202 τριδράχμους κάδους, indicating price, and *PRyl.* 216. 25, al. (ii–iii A.D.), where ἡ τρίδραχμος is said to mean 'the three-drachma tax'; but the word is represented in the papyrus by γ′ and the drachma symbol, which may stand for τριδραχμία (cf. πεντεδραχμία, ἑξαδραχμία in nos. 5, 6 below).

4. The Greek word for tetradrachm[5] takes three forms. The earliest, τετράδραχμον, is first found in *IG* 1². 280⁵⁰ (see below, p. 13), dated in 422–421 B.C., and thereafter in Plato, *Ax.* 366 C, *Michel* 815 (Delos, 364 B.C.) 66, 68, *IG* 2². 1533. 30 (Athens, 338–337 B.C.), *IG* 11. 161 *B* 21, 80 (Delos, 279 B.C.), 162 *B* 17 (278 B.C.), 164 *A* 63 (276 B.C.), and elsewhere. The contracted form τετράαχμον occurs in *IG* 11. 219 *B* 55 (c. 260 B.C.) and 287 *B* 54 (250 B.C.) in the phrase τετράαχμα Πτολεμαϊκά δύο, but later the form τετράχμον[6] is almost always used, at least in inscriptions. Thus in the Delian inventories we find it in *IG* 11. 199 *B* 44 (274 B.C.), 203 *B* 40, 46, 47 (260 B.C.), 223 *B* 29 (262 B.C.), 287 *B* 47 (250 B.C.), *ID* 298 *A* 35 (240 B.C.), and later, in Athenian inventories *IG* 2². 1534. 110 ff. (276–275 B.C.), 203, 231, 252, &c. (232–231 B.C.),

---

[1] Cf. *Didyma*, 471. 7 ἐπιχώριαι (sc. δραχμαί), *SIG* 558. 20 δραχμὰς ἐπιχωρίας.

[2] Babelon 418–19; Schwabacher, *RE* 7A, 104; *Wörterbuch* 702.

[3] For an attempted identification of these coins see Schwabacher, loc. cit. His statement that they 'inschriftlich mehrfach aus Attika bekannt sind' must be modified.

[4] In l. 97 Ἀλεξανδρείας ⊦⊦⊦⊦ and Ἀλεξανδρείας Γ clearly refer to 4 and 5 separate drachmae.

[5] Babelon 417–18; Regling, *RE* 5A, 1072; *Wörterbuch* 688.

[6] Many scholars write τέτραχμον, but according to the normal rules of accentuation the word should be τετράχμον, and this form is preferred by LS, citing *EM* τετράδραχμον· καὶ ἀποβολῇ τοῦ δρ, τετράαχμον· καὶ συναλοιφῇ, τετράχμον· καὶ περισπᾶται. This form I use throughout the present article. A somewhat similar phenomenon is the contraction of the Homeric ἀμφιφορεύς which gave rise to the later form ἀμφορεύς, and that of ἡμιμέδιμνος to ἡμέδιμνος.

Hesperia 11, 245 (229–206 B.C.), and probably *IG* 2². 1537. 11, 15, 16 (late iii B.C.), in an Attic decree, *IG* 2². 839. 55 (221 B.C.), and in a list of the treasures of Amphiaraus at Oropus, *IG* 7. 303 (c. 240 B.C.) 77–91 *passim*.[1] In Latin we find both the full form *tetradrachmum* (Cassius in Cic. *Fam.* 12. 13, 4) and the contracted *tetrachmum* (Livy 34. 52, 6; 37. 46, 3 and 58, 4; 39. 7, 1). In later Greek authors both forms appear. Plutarch, *Sulla* 25, for example, and Pollux 9. 60 write τετράδραχμον, in Diogenes Laertius 7. 18 the manuscripts vary, while in Philodemus, *de ira* 15. 28 Wilke's text τετρά⟨δρα⟩χμον is Cobet's unnecessary correction of the manuscript reading τετράχμον. I need not here repeat the many entries in the lexicographers containing either or both of these forms. The grammarian Ammonius maintained[2] that there is a distinction of meaning between them, τετράχμον μὲν γάρ ἐστι τὸ νόμισμα, τετράδραχμον δὲ τῶν τεσσάρων δραχμῶν, i.e. presumably, the sum, or weight, of 4 drachmae, but the abundant epigraphical evidence does not confirm this differentiation. In papyri the word is surprisingly rare. *PRyl*. 213. 157 has ἐδα(φῶν) συνκεχωρη-(μένων) ἐπὶ (τετραδράχμῳ) ἀργ(υρίου), but the use of the numeral δ' with the drachma-symbol makes the precise form of the word uncertain, and in any case, as the editors note (p. 318), 'it is not clear whether in the present case τετράδραχμος represents a purchase-price, a tax, or the rent on a lease perpetual or temporary'.

LS defines τετράδραχμον as 'silver coin of four drachmas', but, though true in general, this definition is not wholly satisfactory. The first passage cited, *IG* 1². 280. 91, records a τετράδραχμον χρυσοῦν,[3] weighing 7 drachmae 2½ obols, while in *IG* 2². 1534. 91 (276–275 B.C.) we find a [τ]ετράχμον χαλκοῦν among the votives in the Athenian Asclepieum, and the only coin bearing the legend τετράδραχμον is a bronze coin of the 5th century B.C.[4] In *ID* 442 *B* 14, 15 (179 B.C.) we find two τετράχμα ὑπόχαλκα, both of Lysimachus, dedicated in the temple of Apollo. Whether the - - - χμα χαλκᾶ[.] of *IG* 2². 1487. 25 were tetradrachms we cannot say. In the τετράχμον καττιτέρινον of *ID* 1450 *A* 107 Robert sees a coin of tin overlaid with silver (*ENG* 164). Regling describes the tetradrachm as 'die häufigste und mass-

---

[1] See also M. Feyel, *Contribution à l'épigraphie béotienne* 80–84.

[2] Περὶ ὁμοίων καὶ διαφόρων λέξεων, p. 134.

[3] 'Der Goldabguss eines attischen Tetradrachmons' (Regling, *RE* 5A, 1072). It forms item 50 in the inventories of the Parthenon from 422–421 to 412–411 B.C. (*IG* 1². 280, 282–4, 286–8).

[4] K. Regling, *Journ. Intern. Arch. Num.* 11, 243–4, *RE* 5A, 1072; cf. Robert, *ENG* 112–13, who mentions with approval Svoronos's tentative attribution to Palaerus in Acarnania.

gebende Wertstufe im attischen, chiisch-rhodischen, phoinikisch-
tyrischen und ptolemäischen Münzfusse' (*RE* loc. cit.), and its
importance is confirmed by the frequency of its appearance in
inscriptions as well as by the Amphictionic decree passed in the last
quarter of the second century B.C.[1] ἔδοξε τοῖς Ἀμφικτίοσι τοῖς
[ἐλ]θοῦσιν εἰς Δελφούς· δέχεσθαι πάντα[ς] τοὺς Ἕλληνας τὸ Ἀττικὸν
τετράχμ[ον] ἐν δραχμαῖς ἀργυρίου τέταρσι (ll. 2–3); severe penalties are
prescribed for its neglect or infringement (ll. 3–16), and it is enacted
that all the hieromnemons should take to their respective states
sealed copies of the decree (ll. 16–17), and that the secretary should
dispatch copies of it πρὸς πάντας τοὺς Ἕλληνας and should inscribe it
on the Athenian Treasury at Delphi and (perhaps) on the Athenian
Acropolis (ll. 17–19).[2] The fact that various tetradrachms of different
mints and standards circulated in the Greek world made it imperative
to specify Ἀττικὸν τετράχμον in this decree; Livy, it may be noted,
invariably writes *tetrachmum Atticum* (or *tetrachma Attica*) when
enumerating the spoils brought to Rome by victorious generals after
eastern campaigns (see above, p. 13). The Attic tetradrachm was
normally held in high repute, and the words of Zeno of Citium τοῖς
Ἀττικοῖς τετραδράχμοις εἰκῆ κεκομμένοις καὶ σολοίκως[3] express a purely
aesthetic criticism. Among the dedications stored in the Delian
Artemision in 364 B.C. we find eight τετράδραχμα Ἀττικά (*Michel* 815.
61, 68; cf. *IG* 2². 1636. 18), and temple-inventories, Delian and Attic,
include a large number of tetradrachms issued by various cities or
rulers. I cannot here attempt to give a complete list of these, still less
of the many passages in which they are mentioned, but some of them
call for a brief notice with one or two references. Some are named
after the state which issued them, as Ἐφέσιον[4] or Νάξιον;[5] others bear
the name, in adjectival form, of a king or dynast, as Ἀλεξάνδρειον,[6]
Ἀντιγόνειον,[7] Ἀντιόχειον,[8] Λυσιμάχειον,[9] Μαυσώλλειον,[10] Περσικόν,[11]

---

[1] *Delphes* 3 (2). 139 = *SIG* 729. G. Colin dated the decree 'vers le début du 1er siècle
av. J.-C.' (*Delphes* 3 (2), p. 174), and Pomtow (*SIG* loc. cit.) c. 96 B.C., but G. Daux
(*Chronologie delphique* 63) assigns the archonship of Polyon, in which it was passed,
to 121–100 B.C.
[2] The restoration of ll. 17–19 cannot be regarded as certain.
[3] H. von Arnim, *Stoic.* i. 23, no. 81 = Diog. Laert. 7. 18.
[4] *IG* 11. 287 *B* 47 (250 B.C.), *ID* 442 *B* 40 (179 B.C.).
[5] *Michel* 815. 66 (364 B.C.), *IG* 11. 161 *B* 21 (279 B.C.).
[6] *ID* 442 *B* 215 (179 B.C.).
[7] *IG* 2². 1534. 231, 266, 272, 279 (232–231 B.C.).
[8] *IG* 11. 203 *B* 40, 46 (269 B.C.), *ID* 442 *B* 14 (179 B.C.), misspelt Ἀντιμάχειον in
W. H. D. Rouse, *Greek Votive Offerings* 401.
[9] *ID* 442 *B* 14, 15, 17, 93, 203 (179 B.C.), 444 *B* 47 (177 B.C.).
[10] *IG* 11, 161 *B* 21 (279 B.C.), 162 *B* 17 (279 B.C.).
[11] *ID* 1443 *A* i 148; cf. *ENG* 123, n. 5.

Προυσιακόν,[1] Πτολεμαϊκόν,[2] and Φαρνάκειον.[3] Others again bear a title ending in -φόρον, derived from the emblem stamped on their reverse. Among these are the τετράχμα στεφανηφόρα,[4] which, as Robert has shown (ENG 105–35; cf. pp. 8–9 above), are Attic tetradrachms of the 'New Style', on the reverse of which an olive-wreath surrounds the owl and amphora, while the τετράχμα Ἀττικὰ γλαυκοφόρα τῶν πρότερον κοπέντων τοῦ στεφανηφόρου[5] are tetradrachms of the 'Old Style' with an owl, but no wreath, on the reverse. Others, mentioned in the Delian temple inventories of the period of the second Athenian domination (166–87 B.C.) and discussed by Robert, are the τετράχμα καινὰ ταυροφόρα, which he identifies as Eretrian coins of the second century B.C.,[6] and the τετράχμον κιστοφόρον or κισταφόρον or κισσοφόρον,[7] mentioned several times by Cicero and Livy under the name cistophorus.

That τετράδραχμον should sometimes denote a weight rather than a coin was to be expected, despite the silence of LS. Among the passages cited in LS for the coin is IG 7. 3498. 62 (Oropus), but the text runs ταῦτα ἤγαγον τετράχμα γ' καὶ [δραχμ]ήν, showing that here τετράχμον refers to weight and not to value, and it bears the same meaning in Hsch. στατήρ· τετράδραχμον, ἤγουν ἤμισυ οὐγγίας and elsewhere.

The adjective τετράδραχμος is curiously rare. LS cites Arist. Oec. 1347ᵃ33 ὄντος μεδίμνου τῶν ἀλφίτων τετραδράχμου for the meaning 'worth four drachmae', and we may add Photius and 'Suidas'[8] στατήρ· τετράδραχμον νόμισμα, Hsch. στατήρ· τετράδραχμος (cod. τετράγραμμος) and γλαῦξ· νόμισμα Ἀθήνησι τετράδραχμον, unless τετράδραχμον and νόμισμα are nouns in apposition. Τετραδραχμιαῖος is applied to τόκος in IG 5 (1). 1146. 36 (= SIG 748. 36; Gythium, i B.C.), meaning 'of four drachmae' (sc. per mina per month), i.e. 'of 48% per annum'.

5. Pollux 9. 60 speaks of a πεντάδραχμον as coined in Cyrene,[9] and Hero, Spir. 1. 21 (p. 110 ed. Schmidt) tells how εἰς ἔνια σπονδεῖα πεντα-δράχμου νομίσματος ἐμβληθέντος ὕδωρ ἀπορρέει εἰς τὸ περιρραίνεσθαι,

[1] References in ENG 123, n. 2.
[2] IG 11. 161 B 80 (279 B.C.), misspelt Πτολεμαῖον in Rouse, loc. cit. The Πτολε-μαϊκὰ ⌐| of IG 7. 303. 92 (Oropus) may be tetradrachms.
[3] ID 1408 A ii 4 (c. 162 B.C.), 1444 Aa 17 (140 B.C.).
[4] References in ENG 124.   [5] ENG 131–2.
[6] ENG 156–9 (references in 156, n. 4).
[7] ENG 176–7 (references in 177, nn. 5–9).
[8] In Photius and 'Suidas' the manuscript reading is τετράγραμμον.
[9] Cf. BMC Cyrenaica, cclx ff.; Babelon 414–17; Schwabacher, RE 19, 503–4; Wörterbuch 498.

where the coin in question is probably an Egyptian copper coin, the smallest denomination issued.[1] The adjective πεντάδραχμος[2] is used of price in Hdt. 6. 89 νέας πενταδράχμους ἀποδόμενοι, and in ll. 1 and 8 of the epigram of Diophantus quoted below (no. 8), and of value in Arist. *Pol.* 1300b33 συναλλαγμάτων ὅσα δραχμιαῖα καὶ πεντάδραχμα. An alternative spelling is πεντέδραχμος, used of price in *IG* 2². 360 (= *SIG* 304, c. 330 B.C.) 9 μεδίμνους πυρῶν: Π :δράχμους, 30 σῖτον πεντέδραχμον (i.e. at 5 drachmae per medimnus), 68 μεδίμνους Π δράχμους, and 408. 14 [κριθὰς] πεντε[δράχμους].[3] Πεντεδραχμία is a sum of 5 drachmae, not necessarily a coin of that value, in Xen. *HG* 1. 6. 12 πεντεδραχμίαν ἑκάστῳ τῶν ναυτῶν ἐφοδιασάμενος, and in Dinarchus 1. 56 τὴν πεντεδραχμίαν λαβεῖν, 'to receive the 5-drachma allowance', whatever may have been its nature. In Polyaenus 3. 10. 14 τὰς παλαιὰς πεντεδραχμίας[4] must refer to 5-drachma coins, but in a list of leases and sales c. 342 B.C. from the Athenian Agora we find (*Hesperia* 5, 401) in l. 130 a mention of τὴν πεντεδραχμίαν, which B. D. Meritt interprets (p. 411) as 'a five-drachmai tax on the mines', while in ll. 133–5 we find[5] a metic μετασ[χ]|όντα τέλος[6] τῆς πεντεδραχμίας τῆς τῶι Θησε|||[ῖ].

6. Hesychius writes ἔκδραχμον· ἑξάδραχμον, both words presumably being nouns indicating a coin, a value, or a weight.[7] I have not met the former elsewhere, but Aristotle, *Oec.* 1353a18, uses the phrase τιμὴν ἑξαδράχμου. The adjective ἑξάδραχμος (not in LS) occurs in *Oec.* 1347a34, πωλεῖν ἑξάδραχμον, if this reading is correct, 'at the price of 6 drachmae', and in *PHib.* 51. 6 (245 B.C.) Συρίας λάμβανε ἐξ[αδρ]άχμους, 'accept Syrian cloths at six drachmae'. In *PRyl.* 213. 354 (late A.D. ii) we find a heading (ἑξαδράχμου) Φιλαδέλφου, a tax the nature of which is not clear, but the abbreviated form in which it is written makes the precise word uncertain. Ἑξαδραχμία, 'a tax of 6 drachmae', is found in *POxy.* 1457. 2 (4–3 B.C.) τοῖς ἐξειληφόσι τὴν ἑξαδραχμήαν τῶν ὄνων, 'farmers of the six-drachmae tax upon asses'

---

[1] Head, *HN*² 847; Schwabacher, loc. cit.

[2] LS translates 'of the weight or price of five drachmae', but gives no example of the former meaning.

[3] In *PRyl.* 427 fr. 14 (A.D. ii–iii) τῆς (πενταδράχμου), fr. 19 τὴν (πεντάδραχμον) the exact form of the word is uncertain; it might be πενταδραχμία or πεντεδραχμία.

[4] Blume's emendation of the manuscript reading πέντε δραχμάς.

[5] Cf. R. Schlaifer, *Harvard Studies*, 51, 236–8; W. S. Ferguson, *Hesperia*, Suppl. 8, 142–3.

[6] I should have expected τέλους, as in a similar phrase in l. 142.

[7] It is unfortunate that LS gives 'ἔκδραχμος, ον, of six drachmas, Hsch.', with no cross-reference to ἑξάδραχμον. Cf. Babelon 413 (who, citing Hesychius, adds 'mais, sans doute, comme simple expression pondérale') and *Wörterbuch* 265.

(whether on each ass or for a licence to keep asses we cannot say), and this same tax recurs in *POxy*. 1438. 19 (late ii B.C.) and 2414 ii 15, iii 13, though in an abbreviated form.

7. ἑπτάδραχμος, 'at the price of 7 drachmae', occurs in Theocritus, 15. 19 ἑπταδράχμως . . . πέντε πόκως ἔλαβ' ἐχθές, ἅπαν ῥύπον.[1]

8. ὀκτάδραχμος means 'costing 8 drachmae' in ll. 1 and 7 of an arithmetical puzzle expressed as an epigram by Diophantus[2] of Alexandria, *Arithm*. 5. 30 (p. 384 ed. Tannery), which begins

ὀκταδράχμους καὶ πενταδράχμους χοέας τις ἔμιξε.

In *POxy*. 1185. 19 (c. A.D. 200) we find the phrase τὸ ἀργύριον τῆς καλουμένης ὀκταδράχμου, 'the so-called 8-drachma tax', while in *Sammelb*. 7440. 6, 32 εἴ ἐσιν ἐξ ἀμφοτέρων γονέων μητροπολειτῶν ὀκταδράχ[μ]ων the adjective denotes those 'who pay a poll-tax of only 8 drachmae'.[3] I know no epigraphical record of the ὀκτάδραχμον as a coin.

9. ἐννεάδραχμος (not in LS), 'at the price of 9 drachmae', is restored in *IG* 2². 408. 13 (c. 330 B.C.) πυρῶν Σ[ικελικῶν μεδίμνο]υς ΧΧΧΧ χιλίο[υ]ς[4] ἐννεαδρ[άχμους].

10. δεκάδραχμος means 'at the price of 10 drachmae' in Arist. *Oec*. 1352ᵇ15 τοῦ σίτου πωλουμένου δεκαδράχμου, and 'of the value of 10 drachmae' in *BGU* 1134. 7 (i B.C.) ἐράνου δεκαδράχμου. Deca-drachms[5] were coined in early 4th-century Syracuse and in Egypt under Ptolemy II; in Attica there is a single brief issue only, probably to commemorate the victory over the Persians. I cannot recall an epigraphical reference to the δεκάδραχμον (but see n. 7 below).

12. δωδεκάδραχμος[6] means 'at the price of 12 drachmae' in [Dem.] 42. 20 πωλῶν τὰς κριθὰς ὀκτωκαιδεκαδράχμους καὶ τὸν οἶνον δωδεκά-δραχμον, but in *POxy*. 258. 8 (A.D. 86–87?) εἰ ἐξ ἀμφοτέρων γονέων μη[τ]ροπολειτῶν δωδεκαδράχμων ε[ἰσ]ίν it denotes 'one who pays the poll-tax at the reduced rate of 12 drachmae'.[7] Δωδεκαδραχμία (LS p. 2064) occurs in *PMich. Zen*. 60. 2 (248–247 B.C.) ἐνοχλούμεθα ὑπὸ τοῦ

---

[1] LS translates 'worth seven drachmae', but the passage emphasizes the worthless-ness of the goods purchased.

[2] Not Diophantes, as misspelt in *RE* 17, 2387; cf. Babelon 412–13, *Wörterbuch* 471.

[3] Cf. *POxy*. 1473. 3 (A.D. 201).

[4] It is strange that χιλίους should be inserted after ΧΧΧΧ (= 4000).

[5] Babelon 412; Hultsch, *RE* 4, 2413; *Wörterbuch* 124.

[6] Cf. Babelon 411–12, Hultsch, *RE* 5, 1254; *Wörterbuch* 150.

[7] References to this privileged class are frequent in papyri (e.g. *POxy*. 1452 *pm.*, 1552. 14, *PSI* 732, 1230, 1240, &c.), but always in an abbreviated form, usually Ι͞Β͞Σ. In *BGU* 118 ii 9 (ii A.D.) Ι͞Σ (= δεκάδραχμος) occurs in a similar context, but this is probably an error for Ι͞Β͞Σ.

πραγματευομένου τὴν δωδεκαδραχμίαν as a 'tax of 12 drachmae' levied on boats,[1] and it recurs in *PCair. Zen.* 59753. 12, 30.

18. For ὀκτωκαιδεκάδραχμος, 'at the price of 18 drachmae', see no. **12** above.

20. εἰκοσάδραχμος, 'costing 20 drachmae' (LS p. 2065), appears in *PLond.* 1157ᵛ 8 (A.D. 246) ἐπὶ ἁπλῇ τιμῇ εἰκοσαδράχμῳ, and εἰκοσίδραχμος (not in LS) bears the same meaning in *PTeb.* 373. 12 (A.D. 110–11) χαλκοῦ εἰκοσιδράχμου. In a tax-account *POxy.* 2414 iii 1, 18 (ii–iii A.D.) we find sums under the heading κ̄ (δρ.) καὶ μ̄ (δρ.), a 20-drachma tax and a 40-drachma tax, indexed (p. 209) as εἰκοσιδραχμία and τεσσαρακονταδραχμία respectively, but the use of numerals and symbols makes it uncertain what form the words would have taken if written in full. See above, p. 2, n. 5.

30. Here also we find two alternative spellings. Pollux 4. 165 speaks of πυροὶ τριακοντάδραχμοι, 'wheat costing 30 drachmae' a medimnus, but in the inscription of Tolophon relating to the Locrian maidens we find the phrase [ἐκ τοῦ τέλεος μὴ μεῖ]|ον τριακοντοδράχμου ἕνδεκα ἄνδρας (Schwyzer, 366A 21–22; iii B.C.), which, if correctly restored, apparently refers to a census-class of citizens.[2]

40. See above (no. **20**). In *Stud. Pal.* 4. 62. 9 (i A.D.)[3] the 40-drachma tax, indicated by τὴν μ⟨, is written as ⟨τεσσαρακονταδραχμιαίαν⟩, a form accepted without question in LS. But this form is unparalleled, whereas the taxes of 2, 5, 6, and 12 drachmae are occasionally written in full as διδραχμία (see no. **2**), &c., and those of 1, 20, and 40 are usually taken to follow the same pattern. I should therefore prefer to write ⟨τεσσαρακονταδραχμίαν⟩, though ⟨τεσσερακονταδραχμίαν⟩ is also possible.

50. The existence of a 50-drachma coin at Cyrene is asserted by Pollux 9. 60 ἦν δὲ οὐ δραχμὴ νόμισμα μόνον, ἀλλὰ καὶ πεντηκοντάδραχμον[4] [καὶ πεντάδραχμον] παρὰ Κυρηναίοις, and the word recurs in *PCair. Zen.* 59022. 3 (iii B.C.) ἔνεστι μναιεῖα λζ′ καὶ τούτου ἐπαλλαγὴ ⊦ρμη′ πεντηκονταδράχμων (cf. Schwabacher, *RE* 19, 528–9). The corresponding adjective is used by Plato (*Cratylus* 384 B) to indicate the fee charged by Prodicus for a full course of instruction, while for a shortened course one drachma was paid (τὴν δραχμιαίαν ἐπίδειξιν), and in an

---

[1] C. C. Edgar suggested tentatively 'a tax of 12 drachmae on every 100 artabs of the boat's carrying capacity'.

[2] Wilhelm thought that the word might indicate a value (*Jahresh.* 14, 171, 235).

[3] Wessely's revision of *PLond.* 261.

[4] Cf. Babelon 446–7, *Wörterbuch* 499. The spelling πεντεκοντάδραχμον in *RE* 19, 528 is a misprint.

inventory of c. 200 B.C. from the Oropian temple of Amphiaraus we find a number of μαστοὶ πεντηκοντάδραχμοι, 'cups weighing 50 drachmae apiece' (*IG* 7. 3498. 26).

60, 70. ἑξηκοντάδραχμος (not in LS) appears in *CPHerm.* 101. 7 τοῦ γ[ε]νομένου ἀ[ρ]γυρικοῦ ἑξηκονταδρ[ά]χμου μερισμ[οῦ], and ἑβδομηκοντάδραχμος (LS p. 2065) in *PMich. Zen.* 66. 11, 34 (244 B.C.), where it seems to mean 'receiving a monthly salary of 70 drachmae'.

80, 100. In the above-mentioned Oropian inventory, *IG* 7. 3498, ὀγδοηκοντάδραχμος, 'weighing 80 drachmae',[1] occurs in ll. 45, 48, 57, and ἑκατοντάδραχμος, 'weighing 100 drachmae', in ll. 49, 66, and the latter word recurs, with the same meaning, in Galen 13. 491.

200, 300. In an inscription of c. 450 B.C. relating to the finances of the goddess Nemesis at Rhamnus (*SEG* 10. 210) two previously unattested words occur—διακοσιοδράχμων (l. 36) and τριακοσιοδράχμων (ll. 28, 35).[2] These are discussed by P. D. Stavropoullos in Ἀρχ. Ἐφ. 1934–5, 128–32, by M. I. Finley, *Studies in Land and Credit*, 284–5, nn. 39, 43, and most recently by J. Pouilloux, *La Forteresse de Rhamnonte*, 147–50, no. 35. Though their interpretation presents some problems, it seems probable that they indicate two classes of borrowers from the temple funds, owing to the goddess 200 and 300 drachmae respectively.

500. Finally, the term πεντακοσιοδραχμος, 'of the value of 500 drachmae', is applied to an ἔρανος in a Hellenistic dowry-list from Myconos, *SIG* 1215. 6 ἐν τῶι ἐράνωι τ[ῶι] πεντακοσιοδράχμωι, ὃν συνέλεξεν κτλ., and in an Attic ὅρος, J. V. A. Fine, *Horoi* (*Hesperia*, Suppl. 9) 17, no. 28, τοῦ ἐράν[ου τοῦ π]εντακοσιοδρ[άχμου].

Two further compounds call for notice. The half-drachma, ἡμίδραχμον, is, as I have remarked,[3] rarely mentioned except in the phrase τρίτον ἡμίδραχμον (2½ drachmae) explained by Pollux, Photius, Harpocration, and other lexicographers. Pollux 6. 160 includes ἡμίδραχμον among compounds of ἡμι-, and 9. 62 speaks of it as a coin.[4] In the building-accounts of the Erechtheum for 409–408 B.C. we find τετάρτο ἐμι[δ]ράχμο (*IG* 1². 373. 18 = J. M. Paton, *Erechtheum*,

---

[1] Twice the word is written ὀγδοιη-. The translation given in LS, 'amounting to eighty δραχμαί', fails to make clear that the word here refers to weight, not to value, and that the weight in question is that of each cup separately.

[2] See LS pp. 2061, 2108.

[3] *NC* 1947, 13. Regling's article *s.v.* in *RE* 8, 244 consists of only four lines. In the English language, whereas 'halfpenny' and 'half-crown' are in everyday use, the word 'half-shilling' is unknown.

[4] Ἡμιρόδιον is the word normally used for the Rhodian half-drachma, though the feminine form ἡμιρόδια also occurs, e.g. *ID* 1442 B 52–53 (146–144 B.C.) Ῥοδίας ἕξ· … ἡμιρόδια τέτταρα· … Ῥοδίας ὀκτώ· ἡμιροδίας ἕξ.

328), which, on the analogy of τρίτον ἡμίδραχμον, must mean 3½ drachmae. In Galen 13. 674 ἡμίδραχμον denotes a weight, and Eudemus, quoted by Galen 14. 185, uses the phrase ἡμιδράχμοιο ῥοπῆς, where ἡμιδράχμοιο is probably an adjective agreeing with, rather than a noun depending on, ῥοπῆς. The adjective ἡμιδραχμιαῖος (not in LS) occurs in Alexander of Tralles, 8. 446.

There remain μονοδραχμία and μονόδραχμος, translated as 'tax of 1 drachma' and 'of one drachma' respectively by LS, which cites 'PLond. 3. 1157ʳ 6, POxy. 1442. 3 (both iii A.D., abbrev.)' for the former and 'PRyl. 221. 19 (iii A.D.), al.' for the latter. But in none of these passages is μονο- (or any part of it) written, while -δραχμος and -δραχμία are represented only by the drachma-symbol. Thus in PRyl. 221. 19 we have πρὸς (μονόδραχμον), in 427 fr. 14. 10 ἐξ (μονοδρά-χμου), in 427 fr. 17+18. 13 (μονοδράχμου), and in 431 we are simply told that 'the μονόδραχμος charge is mentioned in l. 12'. In POxy. 1442. 3 (A.D. 252) we read ὑπὲρ α (δραχμῆς), which is indexed (p. 335) as μονοδραχμία and translated 'the 1-drachma tax', while in PLond. 1157ʳ 6 the papyrus reads ὑπὲρ ὀνομάτων α⁺ ζευγ' and the commentary states that 'α⁺ may stand for ἀργυρίου or, as Grenfell suggests, for 1 dr.'. Unless, then, there are examples which I have overlooked in which the words are written in full, it would seem that their forms are inferred on the basis of analogy with μοναρταβία and μονάρταβος. But in both examples of μοναρταβία cited in LS, and in a number of others also, the word is represented by the numeral α' and a symbol or abbreviation for ἀρτάβη. Μοναρτάβου is, however, written in full in PSI 1328. 47 (A.D. 201), while an analogous formation is the μονο-δεσμίας of PSI 693. 4 (A.D. 183?).

I have discussed elsewhere[1] the symbols used to denote the drachma, or multiples of the drachma, in the acrophonic numeral systems of the Greek world, and I need not now repeat or summarize what I have there said. Here I call attention to some abbreviations and symbols denoting the word drachma(e) (either of value or of weight) when accompanied by a number (written in words or in acrophonic or alphabetic numerals) indicating the number of drachmae in question, the Greek equivalents, that is to say, of the English £, s., d., or the American $.

The word δραχμή is normally written in full, though occasionally it is wholly omitted.[2] Between these extremes lies a series of abbrevia-tions—ΔP, ΔPA, ΔPAX, ΔPAXM—found most frequently, though

---

[1] BSA 18, 98 ff.; 28, 141 ff.; 37, 236 ff.   [2] For examples see above, p. 6.

not exclusively, in accounts and inventories;[1] sometimes a mark of punctuation calls attention to the abbreviation, e.g. ΔPA: or ΔPAX. I cannot recall an epigraphical example of the use of Δ for this purpose,[2] but ΔP appears in monogram (Fig. 1a) in *IG* 2². 2776 and in a Thasian building-inscription, *IG* 12 (8). 391. 3 (both ii A.D.). Usually the same abbreviation is used consistently throughout an inscription, but in the *catalogi paterarum argentearum* (*IG* 2².

FIG. 1. Drachma-signs.

1553–78) there is a striking absence of uniformity, and the choice of abbreviation apparently depended upon considerations of space or on mere caprice.

Among the symbols used to represent the drachma the commonest is ⊢, which is often prefixed to sums or weights of five drachmae or more expressed in the acrophonic notation; this usage occurs frequently, e.g., in *ID* 442 B (179 B.C.), where we find, for example, 21 drachmae expressed as ⊢ΔΔ⊢ (l. 190).[3] Elsewhere it is followed by alphabetic numerals, as in *IG* 12 Suppl. 556 (Eretria, iii–ii B.C.), where ⊢A, ⊢I, ⊢IE and the like occur, or *SEG* 8. 625 (Egypt) εἰς ἀργύριον λόγον ⊢ ,ητογ′ (see p. 9, n. 6), or Wilcken, *Gr. Ostraka* ii. 371 ⊢ μίαν, 385 ⊢ δεκαοκτώι.[4] Sometimes the cross-bar, instead of being horizontal, slopes upward (Fig. 1b), as in *IG* 12 (3). 327. 14 (Thera, 229 B.C.),[5] *GDI* 3510 (Cnidus, ii B.C.),[6] and *IG* 5 (1). 1498. 5, 9 (Messenia, ii B.C.).[7] In a subscription-list from Caunus (*JHS* 73, 23 ff. = *SEG* 12. 473; ii B.C.?) we find a variant, in which the

[1] For ΔP see, e.g., *IG* 2². 1368. 80, 82, 2776 *passim* (both ii A.D.), for ΔPA *SIG* 46. 9, 11, 13, 15 (Halicarnassus, v B.C.), for ΔPAX *Inscr. Magn.* 100b 35, for ΔPAXM *IG* 5 (2). 357. 139 (Stymphalus; but this may be a case of accidental omission).
[2] In *IG* 9 (2). 1296. 9, 14, 21, 30, 1299. 6, 15 (Azorus) ΔKB denotes δηνάρια κβ′.
[3] By a curious misunderstanding Hultsch wrote (*RE* 5, 1619. 34) "Ῥόδιαι ⊢ΓΗ, d. i. μία πέντε ἑκατόν (δραχμαί) werden angeführt in ... Syll.² 588, 204′, giving an unintelligible interpretation of an obviously corrupt text, now corrected in *ID* 442 B 204.
[4] In *Bull. Inst. Arch. Bulg.* 13, 190 D. Detchev wrote [ἐ]πέδωκεν ⊢ Ἀττικὰς μυρίας, but J. and L. Robert denied the presence of ⊢ (*REG* 61. 169, no. 112).
[5] See above, p. 8.
[6] Mistakenly printed ⊢ in *Michel* 1005.
[7] Printed ⊢ in the majuscule text in *IG* and omitted in the transcript.

down-stroke slopes and the cross-bar is horizontal (Fig. 1c); the numerals which follow are alphabetic, ranging from Ε to Γ. The symbol ⟨ occurs at Delos (*ID* 1521. 24)[1] and possibly also at Sparta (*IG* 5 (1). 19)[2] and Cos (*IGRom*. 4. 1092. 1, 16), though in these last two cases it has been taken to denote the denarius; it is not uncommon in Asia Minor—e.g. at Halicarnassus (*BSA* 50, 99 = *SEG* 16. 645. 12), Panamara (*SEG* 4. 302. 10, 306. 13), Tlos (*TAM* 2. 550–1 *passim*), Cadyanda (ibid. 650), Arneae (ibid. 774. 13), Aperlae (*CIG* 4300 *o*, *v*), and Termessus (*TAM* 3. 3 *B* 21), and in W. Cilicia (*JHS* 12, 234), where it takes a special form (Fig. 1e). A similar sign, in which the second stroke is horizontal (Fig. 1f), occurs at Lindus (*IG* 12 (1). 937), Cyprian Salamis (*BMus. Inscr.* 980. 3, 5), Termessus (*TAM* 3. 590. 17, 18), Eïtha in Batanaea (*LW* 2117), and elsewhere (cf. below, n. 1). Whether the reverse form ⟩, which appears at Termessus (*TAM* 3. 719. 8), represents the drachma or the denarius is uncertain, and the same is true of a symbol (Fig. 1d) resembling the Arabic numeral 3, which occurs at Sparta side by side with ⟨ (see below, note 2). A slightly different symbol (Fig. 1g), probably denoting drachmae, is used in an inscription from Paphos (*BMus. Inscr.* 969). Another common form is that of the St. Andrew's cross, usually differentiated from *chi* by a horizontal bar (Fig. 1h); this serves to denote drachmae or denarii, and it is sometimes difficult, or even impossible, to determine its meaning in a particular case.[3] It indicates drachmae in the statutes of the Athenian society of Iobacchi (*IG* 2². 1368. 38, 55, 90, 161; before A.D. 178), in which four payments are reckoned in δρ(αχμαί), thrice preceded by λεπτοῦ (ll. 80, 99, 110), perhaps in an Athenian record of benefactions (*IG* 2². 2773. 13, 15; c. A.D. 240), in many inscriptions from Termessus in Pisidia (*TAM* 3, p. 355), at Sanaos in Phrygia (*JHS* 17, 414),[4] and elsewhere. In a decree of an

---

[1] So at least it is shown in *ID*; in *BCH* 13, 240 and P. Roussel, *Les cultes égyptiens à Délos*, 204 f., no. 216, it appears as ∠ (Fig. 1f).

[2] In this inscription, which records the regulations of the Spartan festival of the Leonidea, ⟨ occurs thrice and 3 (Fig. 1d) nine times; it is hard to suppose that these signs indicate different values in face of the prize-list of ll. 7–8 [παῖς κα|θαρ]ὸς 3ρ′, ἀγένειος 3ρν′, ἀνὴρ ⟨ς′, where the successive values 100, 150, 200 would naturally be stated in terms of the same coin. W. Kolbe, the editor of *IG* 5 (1), assumed (p. 344) that both alike represented the δηνάριον, and in support of this view it might be urged that in *IG* 5 (1). 18 *B*, an inscription of the same date and relating to the same subject, a fine is prescribed μέχρι 3φ′ (l. 3, where the transcript gives μέχρι ✳φ′), and there is a reference later (l. 13) to ἀσφάλειαι τῶν τρισμυρίων δηναρίων. In a third document of similar content (*IG* 5 (1). 20 *A* 2) Kolbe transcribes ⟨⊐Ε: (i.e. presumably ⟨ξε′) as ✳ε′.

[3] In *IG* 12 (2). 496 (ager Mytilenaeus), for example, Χ ΡΟ is interpreted as (δηνάρια) ρο′, but, if Χ here denotes a value, it might represent (δραχμαὶ) ρο′.

[4] Ἀτικὰς (sic) ✳ ,βφ′, wrongly written as Ἀτικὰς ⟨✳⟩ βφ′ in *IGRom*. 4. 872. 2.

association at Caunus we find five examples of a form (Fig. 1*i*)[1] which the editor regards as unique, but, so far as I can see from the photograph (Pl. I), the symbol is a Χ with slight serifs; a similar sign found at Salkhad (*LW* 1994 = *Princeton Exp. Inscr.* 168; A.D. 325) represents drachmae, not denarii, for it is followed by the words μυρ(ίας) δισχιλίας Σύρας. Finally, in *IG* 12 (2). 67, a Mytilenean decree in Aeolic dialect dating from the reign of Commodus, we find three signs (Fig. 1*j*), preceded in l. 8 by ἀρ|γυρίω and in l. 11 by ταῖς ἐπά|νω εἰρημέναις; that the first sign denotes δράχμαις seems certain, and I cannot doubt that it was followed by a numeral, but the siglum here used presents a problem. W. R. Paton, the editor of *IG* 12 (2), states in a note that it 'ex litteris ΕϹΙ confectum est', but he hazards no conjecture of its value and transcribes in his text (δράχμαις) - -; Lafaye in *IGRom.* 4. 45 writes (δράχμαις) . . without comment, and Schwyzer in *DGE* 627 has (δραχμαῖς εσι') with the note 'post vocem (δρ.) siglo scriptam est siglum numeri ex litteris εσι confectum (IG)'. But this is unsatisfactory for several reasons: (1) I cannot agree that the sign in question is a monogram composed of ΕϹ and Ι; throughout the inscription these letters are invariably represented by apicated forms of Ε Ϲ and Ι, and there is no trace of the intrusion of any 'lunate' forms; (2) the expression of a number in such monogrammatic form is, so far as I know, unparalleled in Greek epigraphy; (3) it is highly improbable that the numerals εσι would occur in that order rather than the normal σιε' or the rare σει'; (4) these numerals give a total value of 215, which is hardly credible in the present context, which prescribes the penalty for the infringement of a decree of Council and People. Professor G. Klaffenbach has, with characteristic helpfulness and promptitude, lent me the squeeze of this inscription from the Berlin collection, for which I owe him my warmest thanks. This proves that the stone bears the signs shown in Fig. 1*k*. The curved stroke on the left I take as the sign that the following numeral represents thousands: this is normally straight, but is frequently curved by way of ornament.[2] But what is the numeral to which it is attached? I can see only two possible answers, ͵ε and ͵θ, giving totals of 5,000 and 9,000 drachmae. Both present difficulties, and it would seem that the designer or the engraver allowed his imagination free play not only in the unique drachma-sign, but also in the numeral-letter. If this represents θ, it is unlike

---

[1] *JHS* 74, 87–88, ll. 26, 29, 33, 34, 46.
[2] See, for example, J. R. S. Sterrett, *Epigraphical Journey* 397.

the form used elsewhere in the inscription, which has a complete circle and within it a short apicated bar, while here the circle is incomplete and the cross-bar extends right across it; if, on the other hand it represents ϵ, it presents us with an apicated version of a 'lunate' form, which survives in modern typography as 'e'. Of the two alternatives I prefer the latter.

MARCUS N. TOD